Heinrich Heine, James Geikie

Songs and Lyrics

Heinrich Heine, James Geikie

Songs and Lyrics

ISBN/EAN: 9783744780155

Printed in Europe, USA, Canada, Australia, Japan

Cover: Foto ©Thomas Meinert / pixelio.de

More available books at **www.hansebooks.com**

SONGS AND LYRICS

BY HEINRICH HEINE

AND OTHER GERMAN POETS

Done into English Verse

BY JAMES GEIKIE

Author of 'The Great Ice Age,'
'Prehistoric Europe,' etc.

EDINBURGH: JAMES THIN
Publisher to the University
1887

To my Wife

'A translator dyes an author, like an old stuff, with a new colour, but can never give it the lustre of the first tincture, as silks that are twice dyed lose their glosses, and never receive a fair colour. He is a small factor that imports books of the growth of one language into another, but it seldom turns to account; for the commodity is perishable, and the finer it is, the worse it endures transportation, as the most delicate of Indian fruits are by no art to be brought over. . . . His labours are like dishes of meat twice drest, that become insipid, and lose the pleasant taste they had at first. He differs from an author as a fiddler does from a musician, that plays other men's compositions, but is not able to make any of his own.'—BUTLER.

Note by the Translator.

ALL the critics agree that Heine's verse is untranslatable. And yet the present is as far from being the first as it is unlikely to be the last rash attempt to accomplish the impossible. In explanation of his temerity the Translator may be allowed to state that all the renderings given in this little volume were done for his own amusement in those 'brave days of youth,' when difficulties and impossibilities are hardly recognised. Some apology for their publication is perhaps required; but if his rhymes do not justify themselves, the Translator knows of no excuse for their appearance that is likely to pass muster. While he has endeavoured in these versions of some of Heine's most characteristic Songs and Lyrics to interpret the poet's language literally, he has at the same time done his best to follow the rhythm and rhymes of the German. Whether he has succeeded in retaining even the slightest flavour of the original, or in reproducing any far-off echo of the music of the immortal *Buch der Lieder*, others must judge.

The Poems in Part II. have not been selected upon any principle. While not a few of them have already been Englished, a considerable number, it is believed, appear now for the first time in our tongue.

EDINBURGH, *July 8, 1887.*

CONTENTS.

PART I.

The Book of Songs

BY HEINRICH HEINE.

PREFACE TO THE THIRD EDITION (1839), . . Page 1

YOUTH'S SORROWS.—1817-1821.

DREAM PICTURES.

I once would dream of love,—of sunny hair, . . .	3
An eerie, thrilling dream I dream'd, ...	3
Why doth my blood so madly flow?	7
In sweetest dreams, by silent night, ...	8
Thou dark, scowling fellow, I've paid thee, I trow! .	11
I wander'd back from my darling's bower, . . .	14
I fell asleep, and quietly slept, ...	20
The ghastly spectres grieve me, ...	21

SONGS.

Up I start at morning, crying, ...	23
O'erhead the leaves are shaking, ...	23
Thy little hand lay on my heart, my fair! . . .	24
Cliff and castle, downward glancing, ...	24
First methought I'd sink before it, ...	25
Fain would I deck this book of mine, ...	25

CONTENTS.

ROMANCES.

Every heart is filled with sorrow,	Page 27
Sadly adown the valley rode,	27
On the hill-top, silent, darkling,	28
My grannie bewitch'd poor Lizzie one day,	29
Two grenadiers, in Russia ta'en,	30
Up! up! good knave, go saddle thy steed,	32
I go not alone, my lady fair!	32
'Donna Clara! Donna Clara!'	33
The midnight hour was drawing on,	39
Sad in my heart is written,	40
I lean'd against the bending mast,	41
Sir Ulrich rides through the forest glade,	42
That lovely siren long will haunt me,	44
Golden ducats, once my own,	45
Hear'st thou not these strains of wonder,	46
When spring-time comes with its sunny sheen,	47

LYRICAL INTERMEZZO.—1822-1823.

There once was a knight, wan and thin was his cheek,	49
'Twas in the glorious month of May,	50
Flowers from my tears are springing,	51
The rose, the lily, the dove, the sun,	51
When I look into thine eyes,	51
In dreams methinks I see thy face,	52
In the dainty cup of the lily,	52
All through the ages shine they,	53
Away! away! with me, love!	53
The lotus flower a-weary,	54

CONTENTS.

Thou lov'st me not, thou lov'st me not,	Page 54
O swear not! only kiss and kiss,	55
Upon thine eyes, beloved mine,	55
Little darling, tell me truly,	56
I'll not reproach thee! though my heart should break,	56
Yes! thou art wretched, and no plaint I make,	57
There merry music soundeth,	57
And hast thou then forgotten fully,	57
And if each little blossom,	58
Why are the roses so wan and pale?	58
They've plained to thee and lamented,	59
The linden blossom'd, the nightingale sung,	60
The earth had been long a niggard of beauty,	60
Her eyes are violets wet with due,	61
The world is fair and the heavens are blue,	61
My love, when thou art gone away,	61
In the North a pine stands lonely,	62
Ah! were I but the stool so light,	62
Since my loved one went afar,	63
The little songs I utter,	63
The cits in their Sunday dresses,	64
Dreams of old times forgotten,	64
A youth he loved a maiden,	65
When the song she sang so sweetly,	66
I dreamt of a wan and tearful face,	66
In a little skiff I rested,	67
From olden legends springing,	67
On a sunny summer morning,	68
In its dim mysterious glory,	68
They worried me, and drove me,	69
Warm summer, love, is lying,	70

When dearest friends are parting,	Page 70
At the tea-table love was the topic,	70
And if my songs are poison'd,	71
I dream'd again the same old dream,	72
In dreams I fell a-weeping,	72
In the dreams of night I see thee,	73
Wild is the night and eerie,	73
The trees in the autumn wind rustle,	73
A star falls in the darkness,	74
Night lay upon my eyelids,	75
The old songs, wild and wicked,	77

THE RETURN HOME.—1823-1824.

In my life so dark and dreary,	78
I know not what sad fate befalls me,	78
Sad is my heart and weary,	79
Sad through the wood I wander,	80
We sat by the fisherman's cottage,	81
Thou pretty fisher-maiden,	82
The storm plays weird dance music,	82
The clouds are creeping downward,	83
Far on the dim horizon,	84
'Tis night, not a sound through the streets doth go,	85
How canst thou sleep so quietly?	85
A maiden slept in her chamber,	86
I stood in dark dreams gazing,	87
The years are waxing and waning,	87
Methought that the moon shone mournfully,	87
What means this lonely tear-drop,	88

The sickle moon of autumn,	Page 89
It rains, and snows, and blusters,	90
They tell me I am grieving,	91
Has she then no notice taken,	91
They both were in love, but neither,	92
When I told you the sorrowful life I had led,	92
I call'd the devil and he came,	92
My little one, we were children,	93
My heart within me is a-weary,	94
As yon moon in brightness breaketh,	95
Heart of mine, be not dejected,	96
So fair, so pure, so gentle,	96
When on my couch I lay me,	96
Maiden, with the lips so rosy,	97
Canst thou not read in my wan cheek,	97
Worthy friend, thou art in love!	98
When I with you would tarry,	98
Thine eyes are sapphires, sweet and bright,	99
In one single word, could I utter,	99
Diamonds and pearls are thine, love!	100
They counsell'd me, and well advised me,	100
How in youth love's glow hath brought me,	101
On the walls of Salamanca,	101
Where dreamlike stretch the houses,	102
Ah! these are yet the very eyes,	103
Death is the night, so cool, so calm,	103
Say, where is thy maiden sweet?	104
At the window stands the mother,	104
I am the Princess Ilse (from the *Tour in the Harz*)	107

LATER POEMS.

When, Germany, of thee I think,	Page 109
There was a king, an old king.	110
Now spring's blue eyes are peeping,	111
The waters glitter and glide away,	111
Sweetly in my heart doth ring,	112
Where then shall I rest for ever (*posthumous verses*),	112

PART II.

Miscellaneous Pieces

BY VARIOUS GERMAN POETS.

Spring Song (*Wilhelm Müller*),	117
A Change (*Goethe*),	118
New Life (*Bürger*),	119
No Answer (*Robert Reinick*),	120
The Secret will out (*Emanuel Geibel*),	120
Secrecy (*Carl Dräxler-Manfred*),	121
Parting (*Volkslied*),	122
Presence in Absence (*Goethe*),	123
The Soldier's Love (*Wilhelm Hauff*),	124
An Evil Conscience (*Moritz Graf Strachwitz*),	125
The Three Roses (*Volkslied*),	126
Desolation (*Albert Traeger*),	128
The Old Oak-tree (*Volkslied*),	128
Unrest (*Emanuel Geibel*),	129

CONTENTS.

Calm after Storm (*Moritz Graf Strachwitz*), . Page	130
Winter Dreams (*Eduard Ferrand*), ...	131
The Nun (*Volkslied*), ...	132
The Landlady's Daughter (*Uhland*), . . .	134
Love's Legacy (*Emanuel Geibel*), ...	135
Dame Nightingale (*Volkslied*), ...	136
The Laurel and the Rose (*Ernst Schulze*), . .	137
The Water Lilies (*August Schnetzler*), . . .	138
The Rosebud (*Friedrich von Sallet*), . . .	139
The Dying Flower (*Friedrich Rückert*), . .	140
The Maiden and the Butterfly (*R. C. Wegener*), .	143
The Days of the Roses (*Otto Roquette*), . .	144
The Duet (*Robert Reinick*), ...	144
SONG: How gladly at thy feet, love (*Moritz Graf Strachwitz*), ...	145
Wandering (*Emanuel Geibel*), ...	146
The Apprentice setting out (*Uhland*), . .	147
Hidden Pain (*Volkslied*), ...	148
The Linden-Tree (*Wilhelm Müller*), . .	149
The Elder-Tree (*Otto Roquette*), . . .	150
Evening Song (*Friedrich Rückert*), . . .	151
Autumn (*Hermann Lingg*), ...	152
Onward (*Heinrich Zeise*), ...	153
Longings (*C. A. Mahlmann*), ...	154
The Little Sister (*Volkslied*), . . .	156
The Trial of Love (*Volkslied*), . . .	158
The Dark Brown Nixie (*Volkslied*), . .	159
The Inexorable Captain (*Volkslied*), . . .	160
The Poet King (*Joseph Freiherr von Eichendorff*), .	162
The Captive Knight (*J. C. von Zedlitz*), . .	162
The Two Coffins (*Justinus Kerner*), . . .	163

CONTENTS.

The Poet's Consolation (*Justinus Kerner*),	Page 164
The Castle by the Sea (*Uhland*),	165
The Ancestral Vault (*Uhland*),	166
The Blind King (*Uhland*),	167
The Nibelunger's Treasure (*Volkslied*),	170
The Pope and the Sultan (*Volkslied*),	171
Crambambuli (*Studentenlied*),	172
The Man in the Cellar (*K. Müchler*),	174
Comfort at Parting (*A. F. F. von Kotzebue*),	175
Fiducit (*Studentenlied*),	177
Chateau Boncourt (*Adalbert von Chamisso*),	178
To the Fatherland (*Nicolaus Lenau*),	179
Rhine Song (*Wolfgang Müller*),	181

IMITATIONS.

Butterflies, Butterflies, tell me true,	185
Down where the aspens quiver,	185
Long ago, when my heart was young,	186

ERRATA.

Page 61, line 2 from top, *for* violet *read* violets.
,, 112, line 8 from bottom, *for* sing *read* ring.

PART I.

From 'The Book of Songs'

BY

HEINRICH HEINE.

PREFACE.

It is the fairy wood of old,
   With bloom of the lindens haunted;
The wondrous sheen of the moon, I ween,
   My heart and soul enchanted.

I wander'd on, and as I roam'd
   Soft notes o'erhead kept ringing—
It is the nightingale, of love
   And love's wild sorrow singing.

With love and yearning, tears and smiles,
   Her tender breast is shaken;
Her jubilant grief, her joyous sobs
   Old dreams in my heart awaken.

I wander'd on, and as I roam'd
   Saw glimmering before me
A mighty castle in a glade—
   High soar'd its turrets o'er me.

Closed were the windows, all was sad,
   And not a sound did waken;
It seem'd as death itself abode
   Within these walls forsaken.

Before the door there crouch'd a sphynx,
   Alluring and yet gruesome;
A lion's body and paws it had,
   A woman's head and bosom:

A beautiful woman, whose white cheek told
    Of passionate love and tender;
The dumb lips seem'd to smile, as they
    Would fain their sweets surrender.

So witchingly sang the nightingale—
    How could my heart resist it?
I kiss'd that lovely face, and knew
    My fate was seal'd when I kiss'd it.

Life through the marble 'gan to thrill—
    Soft sighs and balmy blisses—
With eager, panting thirst she drank
    The glow of my hot kisses.

She almost drank my breath away;
    To her panting bosom she bore me—
Her panting, craving bosom—and deep
    The claws of the lion tore me.

O rapturous torment! O blissful woe!
    The pain, like the joy, stupendous—
The kisses thrill'd to my inmost heart,
    But the clutch of the claws was tremendous!

The nightingale sang: 'O beautiful Sphynx,
    O loved one, say how this is—
Why dost thou mingle the pains of death
    With all thy rapturous kisses?

'O beautiful Sphynx, this riddle read,
    And in my maze bestead me;
I've ponder'd it many a thousand years,
    But ever its meaning fled me.'

YOUTH'S SORROWS.

DREAM PICTURES.

„Mir träumte einst von wildem Liebesglühn."

I ONCE would dream of love,—of sunny hair,
   And mignonette and myrtle intermingled,
   Of sweet red lips, and bitter words that tingled,
Of many a mournful song and plaintive air.

Ah me! those dreams have long ago departed,
   My dearest vision never comes again;
   Love's anguish and wild joy and throbbing pain
Live only in these numbers broken-hearted.

Thou, orphaned song! art left: do thou too hie,
   And seek again for me that long-lost vision;
   And shouldst thou find it, be thy gentle mission
To greet that light shade with an airy sigh.

„Ein Traum, gar seltsam schauerlich."

AN eerie, thrilling dream I dream'd,
Half fearful and half sweet it seem'd.
That eerie dream I can't forget,
My troubled heart throbs wildly yet.

It was a garden wondrous fair,
And fain was I to wander there;
Sweet flowers a many look'd at me,
And all my spirit danced with glee.

The birds i' the twinkling boughs above
Sang many a cheery song of love;
I' the golden light the red sun threw
The flowerets bright and brighter grew.

Rich herbs with many a balmy sigh
Scented the breeze that flutter'd by;
Around me all was fresh and fair—
'Twas light and laughter everywhere.

Deep in the heart of that good land
I saw a marble fountain stand,
And by its marge a maiden bright,
Washing a vestment snowy white.

Her eyes were soft, her cheeks were fair,
And rich the gleam of her yellow hair;
And while I gazed on her, methought
I knew, and yet I knew her not.

The lovely maiden sped her toil,
And croon'd a wondrous song the while:
'Hasten, hasten, waterflow!
Wash the linen white as snow.'

Then to her side I softly drew,
And whisper'd low: 'O tell me true,
Thou lovely maiden, sweet and dear,
For whom is this white vestment here?'

YOUTH'S SORROWS.

Quickly she answer'd: 'Ready be!
I wash thy winding-sheet for thee;'
And hardly had these words been said
Ere like a mist the vision fled.

Enchanted still, methought I stood
Within a wild and darksome wood;
To heaven the forest tower'd confused,
And marvelling there, I mused, and mused.

But hark! what distant echo wakes?—
A hatchet-stroke the silence breaks!—
Far through the wood the sound I chase,
And reach at last an open space.

There, in the midst of that green glade,
A mighty oak-tree casts its shade:
And lo! the self-same maid appears,
And 'gainst the oak a hatchet rears.

With stroke on stroke she sped her toil,
And swung her axe, and croon'd the while:
'Iron bright, iron best,
Shape me quick an oaken chest.'

Then to her side I softly drew,
And whisper'd low: 'O tell me true,
Thou wondrous lovely maiden mine,
For whom dost shape this oaken shrine?'

Quickly she cried: 'The end draws nigh;
To shape thy coffin here am I.'
And hardly had these words been said,
Ere like a mist the vision fled.

Now only a wan waste and wide
Stretch'd drearily on every side:
I felt I knew not how, and stood
To secret shuddering subdued.

As on I wander'd, far away
A white streak glimmer'd like a ray:
I hasten'd o'er the moorland bare
To reach it—and the maid was there.

On the wide heath-land stood the maid,
And deep in earth she dug her spade;
Scarce dared I look, for in my dream
Fearful, though lovely, did she seem.

Eager the maiden sped her toil
And croon'd a wondrous song the while:
'Shovel, shovel, sharp and tried,
Dig a hollow deep and wide.'

Then to her side I softly drew,
And whisper'd her: 'O tell me true,
Thou lovely maiden, sweet and dear,
What means this gaping hollow here?'

Quickly she answer'd: 'Silent be!
A deep, cool grave I've dug for thee.'
And while the maiden thus replied,
The hollow, yawning, open'd wide.

As towards the brink I fearful drew,
An icy shiver thrill'd me through;
Into the chasm that yawn'd and quaked
Sudden I stumbled—and awaked.

„**Was treibt und tobt mein tolles Blut?**"

WHY doth my blood so madly flow?
What sets my fever'd heart aglow?
My hot blood boils and frets and fumes,
And this wild glow my heart consumes.

My hot blood boils since that weird dream
When gloomy Night's dark Son did seem
To come to me at midnight grim,
And draw me panting after him.

To a brave house he brought me, where
'Mid tapers' gleam and torches' flare,
And sounding harp, and mirth, and all,
I softly stepp'd into the hall.

It was a wedding-feast, I knew:
The merry guests to table drew:
I stood the happy pair beside—
O woe! my loved one was the bride.

It was my darling, none but she;
Her mate a stranger was to me.
And close behind the lady's chair
I shrinking stood in mute despair.

The music rang; I took no part
I' the joyous din that chill'd my heart:
The bride's sweet glances spoke her bliss,
The bridegroom press'd her hands in his.

The bridegroom fill'd a beaker up,
And drank thereout, and pass'd the cup:
Sweetly she smiled her love to thank—
O woe! it was my blood she drank.

The bride took up an apple fair,
And gave it to the bridegroom there:
He cut it with his knife apart—
O woe! it was my very heart.

Her look was soft, his gaze was warm,
He boldly clasp'd her yielding form,
And kiss'd her cheek so bright of blee—
O woe! but icy Death kiss'd me.

My tongue like lead in silence lay,
A single word I could not say:
The din uprose, 'twas revel all,
The happy pair danced through the hall.

Whilst cold and lifeless thus I stood,
The dancers wheel'd in merry mood:
The bridegroom spoke a low, soft word,
Then blush'd yet smiled the bonnie bird.

„Im süßen Traum, bei stiller Nacht."

IN sweetest dreams, by silent night,
There came to me with magic might,
With magic might, my dearest dear,
Into my little chamber here.

YOUTH'S SORROWS.

I gazed, and to my earnest gaze
A gentle smile lit up her face;
And as she smiled my heart beat high,
And forth these words in tumult fly:

'My sweet, take all, take all from me,—
Gladly I'll yield up all to thee,—
Wilt thou, lock'd in my arms, but stay
From midnight till the break of day.'

The dear one look'd upon me fain,
A strange, sad look of love and pain:
And, gazing thus, cried earnestly:
'O give thy hope of heaven to me!'

'My life, my youth, yea, all that's mine,
To thee I'll eagerly resign,
But ah! sweet maiden, as I live,
My hope of heaven I cannot give!'

The words were bold and swiftly said,
Yet ever fairer bloom'd the maid,
And, gazing still, cried earnestly:
'O give thy hope of heaven to me!'

And aye these words rang in my ear,
And smote my inmost heart with fear;
In fire my very soul they sheathed;
Panting I lay, and hardly breathed.

And now fair angels to my gaze
Stood shining in a golden haze,
When up there came, with shriek and shout,
A black and horrid goblin rout.

They struggled with the angel band,
They drove away the angel band;
And then I saw the goblin crew
In clouds and darkness vanish too.

I long'd to fade in joy away,
My loved one on my bosom lay;
Close crept she like a little roe,
Yet wept the while with bitter woe.

She wept—and why full well I wist!
To peace her rosy lips I kiss'd:
' O stay those bitter tears of thine,
And yield thee to this love of mine!

' Yield to the love that yearns for thee!'
Then sudden froze my blood in me:
Earth trembled from its depths profound,
A yawning chasm rent wide the ground.

Out from the chasm the goblin trail
Rose black and grim; my love grew pale,
And, fading in my arms, my own,
My loved one, left me all alone!

In a dark ring the goblin rout
Danced round me now with shriek and shout;
They hustled me, they clutch'd me tight,
And scoff'd and jeer'd with all their might.

And ever nearer me they come,
And ever these fearful words they hum—
' Thou 'st given thy hope of heaven away,
And ours thou art for ever and aye!'

„Nun haft du das Kaufgeld, nun zögerſt du doch?"

Thou dark, scowling fellow, I've paid thee, I trow!
So prithee, begone! What's keeping thee now?
Here I in my snug little chamber abide,
Mirk midnight draws near, and I wait but the bride.

Damp, shuddering winds from the churchyard sigh—
Have you seen, clammy winds, my wee bride passing by?
Then all round about me wild, wan faces press,
And bow to me, nodding and grinning, 'O yes!'

Come, out with thy message! what is thy desire,
Thou ugly black scoundrel, in livery of fire?
'My most gracious lady doth here notify
That, drawn by her dragons, she comes by and by.'

Dead master of mine, what wind has brought thee?
Dear grey little mannie, what wantest with me?
He looks in my face, touch'd and sad as he may,
Then shakes his old head, and goes on his way.

Why whimpers that shaggy dog, wagging his tail?
Why glares the black tom-cat, with eyes fierce and fell?
And why howl the women with long, streaming hair?
And why sings old nursey my cradle-song there?

Old nurse, bide at home with that sing-song and prate,—
That hush-a-by-baby is rather too late!
To-day is my wedding—see! many a guest
Already approaches, trick'd out in his best.

Just look!—My dear sirs, now I call it polite
With heads 'stead of hats in your hands to alight!
Ye clattering-boned fellows in gallows array,
What's kept ye?—the wind has been sleeping all day.

On her broomstick an old witch comes riding to me—
Ah, bless me, my mother! thy son I must be.
The blue lips twitch in her wan, wither'd face—
'For ever, amen!' are the words that she says.

Twelve scrannel-piped singers make piteous appeals,
A blind fiddler-wife limps in at their heels;
On a grave-digger's back next clumsily jogs
A clown through my room in his bright-colour'd togs.

Now twelve nuns, all dancing and skipping, advance,
The leering old abbess aye leading the dance;
Next twelve wanton priests, who, without any qualm,
Strike up a vile song to the tune of a psalm.

Old clothesman! don't bawl yourself blue in the face;
Your fur-coat in hell would be quite out of place;
Down there fire costs nothing, fed through the long years,
Not with wood, but with bones of paupers and peers.

The flower-girls, crooked and bent though they be,
Tumble head over heels in the room beside me;
With grasshopper legs and owlish-like gibs—
Give up, I beseech ye, that rattling of ribs!

Now surely all hell is let loose for the night;
The rout swarms hither in tumult and fight;
E'en the waltz of damnation resounds far and near—
Hush! hush! for my loved one will shortly be here.

Hush! hush! ye vile scum, or pack off to your lair—
I hardly can hear myself speak, I declare!
Dear me, there's a carriage my dwelling before—
Old cookie, where are you? Quick—open the door!

Now welcome, my darling! how dost thou, my fair?
And you, Mister Parson, pray do take a chair;
With your horse-hoofs and tail, Mister Parson, you see
Your humble and dutiful servant in me!

Sweet bride, why art thou so silent and white?
The parson is ready to wed us to-night.
I'll pay him his dues, dear as blood though they be;
They are nothing when weigh'd 'gainst the winning of thee.

Kneel down then, sweet bride; kneel down by my side!—
There kneels she, there sinks she—O rapturous tide!
She sinks on my heart, all wild in its nest;
I clasp her with shuddering joy to my breast.

Now o'er us the golden locks waver and shine,
Now warmly beateth her heart against mine.
With rapture and woe to and fro they are driven,
And soar away into the bosom of heaven.

And there up above, in God's holy height,
Our hearts are swimming in rapture and light;
But ah! on our heads, as a terrible brand,
Has hell laid in triumph a withering hand.

The dark son of night and terror, no less,
Is the priest who comes our union to bless;
From a blood-stain'd book he murmurs the verse,
His prayer is blaspheming, his blessing a curse.

But hark! how it crashes, and hisses, and howls,
As when thunder rattles and wild ocean scowls;
And see! in the gloom a sudden blue blaze—
'For ever, amen!' the old mother says.

"Ich kam von meiner Herrin Haus."

I WANDER'D back from my darling's bower,
In frenzy and dread, at the midnight hour,
And as I stole through the churchyard grey
The solemn tombs nid-nodded away.

The minstrel's tombstone is nodding, methinks,—
Yet no! 'tis the moon that flickers and blinks!
Hush! a whisper: 'Dear brother, I come! I come!'
And a pale weird shade rises out of the tomb.

'Tis the ghost of the minstrel himself I see—
Perch'd high on the top of his tomb sits he;
The strings of his lute he strikes with a will,
And sings as he plays right hollow and shrill:

'Dull chords and sad, know ye still the lay,
The lay that once the heart could sway,
    And to frenzy could inflame it?
'Tis the joy of heaven, sing the angel choir;
'Tis the woe of hell, howl the devils in fire—
    And *love* poor mortals name it.'

The sound of that word is scarcely gone
Ere the graves begin to open and yawn;
And shadowy forms in crowds draw near
And screech round the singer shrill and clear—

> 'Love, O love, it was thy might
> Sent to bed each luckless wight,
> And his eyelids shut up tight,—
> Why then waken us to-night?'

Thus howl they, and hiss, and moan, and groan,
And patter and clatter round the stone,
Where the minstrel sits and wildly sings
As he strikes again the quivering strings—

> 'Brave! bravo! ye have heard!
> Mad as ever,
> Ah! ye never
> Can resist my magic word.
> Since in our dark chamber we
> Quiet as mice must ever be,
> To-night we'll freak it merrily!—
> Stop a bit!—
> Is there no man here to see?—
> Noodles were we in the world,
> By our passion madly hurl'd
> Into love's fierce flaming pit!
> Now to freak it well and fully,
> Each one here shall tell us truly
> How it happen'd in his case—
> How o'erborne
> He was torn
> In love's frantic, furious chase.'

Then, light as the wind, skips out from the throng
A thin, meagre shadow, humming this song:—

' A tailor was my master,
　　With needle and with shears;
Than I none plodded faster
　　With needle and with shears.

His daughter play'd her part, Sir,
　　With needle and with shears;
And prick'd me to the heart, Sir,
　　With needle and with shears.'

Then laugh'd all the ghosts with a merry shout;
As grave as a judge a second stepp'd out:—

　　'By Rinaldo Rinaldini,
　　Schinderhanno, Orlandini,
　　And especially Charles Moor,
　　As my model men I swore.

　　And since they had loved and courted,
　　So I too myself disported;
　　Dreaming of the fairest maid,
　　I was like to lose my head.

　　Sighing, cooing, hard and harder,
　　I went mad with love and ardour,
　　And my thoughtless fingers slid
　　'Neath my neighbour's pocket-lid.

　　But the street-watch used me badly,
　　And my tears were flowing sadly,
　　Till I dried up all my grief
　　In my neighbour's handkerchief.

Then facetious bailiffs chased me,
Caught me kindly and embraced me;
And in Bridewell, free from harms,
There I found a mother's arms.

Full of love, and musing sweetly,
There much wool I spun discreetly,
Till Rinaldo's shade came by,
Snatch'd my soul, and—here am I!'

Then laugh'd all the ghosts with a merry shout.
Berouged and bedizen'd a third stepp'd out:—

' As king of the boards I spouted,
   A lover was my rôle;
" Ye gods!" I bellow'd and shouted,
   And sigh'd with all my soul.

To " Mortimer "—my best part, Sir,—
   Maria was fair and fit;
But though I play'd from the heart, Sir,
   She never would see it a bit.

" Maria!" cried I in a stagger
   Of wild despairing, and fell—
For, nimbly plying a dagger,
   I'd stabbed myself rather too well.'

Then laugh'd all the ghosts with a merry shout.
In coarse white jacket a fourth stepp'd out:—

' The Professor held forth from his place in the College,
   And soundly the while I snoozed on a bench;
From his daughter I'd rather been gathering knowledge—
   She was such a neat little, sweet little wench.

Ah! oft from her windows she'd nod me a greeting,
  My blossom of blossoms, the light of my life:
My blossom of blossoms was pluck'd, and my sweeting—
  A mean, money'd philistine had her to wife.

Then cursed I the women and rogues with long purses,
  And mix'd devil's drugs in my wine rather free;
And, drinking with Death, while I pour'd out my curses,—
  "Your health! I'm your comrade for ever," cried he.'

  Then laugh'd all the ghosts with a merry shout.
  A fifth with a rope round his neck stepp'd out:—

    ' A purse-proud Count sat over his wine,
    And bragg'd of his daughter and jewels so fine.
    I heed not the jewels, Sir Count, that are thine,
    I had rather thy dear little daughter were mine.

    Now both, he thought, were safe as could be,
    For bolts, and bars, and knaves had he.
    But what were his doors and knaves to me?—
    I had perfect faith in my ladder, d' ye see?

    Then up to the dear one's lattice I went,
    When some one below to a curse gave vent:
    "Fair and softly, my lad; I'm coming up too;
    I love the jewels as well as you."

    Thus jeer'd the Count as he grasp'd me tight,
    And his knaves stood round and laugh'd outright;
    "Deuce take ye, rascals! no thief I be;
    I was only taking my love to me."

Explain as I would, it was no use;
They soon got ready a rope and noose:
And the sun when he rose did wondering stare
As I swung about in the morning air.'

Then laugh'd all the ghosts with a merry shout.
And a sixth with his head in his hand stepp'd out:—

'To hunt i' the wood love drove me out,
With gun in hand I crept about;
A raven croaking in a tree
"Head off! head off!" stood eyeing me.

O that I saw a little dove!
For I would take it to my love,—
Thus musing, every bush and tree
My sportsman's eye scann'd narrowly.

But hush! what low sweet cooing 's this?—
Two turtle-doves I hope it is:
I cock my gun, and steal hard by,
And there—my only love I spy!

My dove, my bride, with all her charms,—
A stranger clasps her in his arms!
Old gun, be steady! fail me not!—
The stranger on the ground lay shot.

Soon headsmen in the wood were seen,
Walking away with me between;
The raven croaking in a tree
"Head off! head off!" stood eyeing me.'

Then laugh'd all the ghosts with a merry shout.
And last the minstrel himself stepp'd out:—

 'I once sang a song, love's token;
  That beautiful song is o'er:
 When the heart within me was broken,
  Song left me evermore.'

Then louder and weirder their laughter rang out,
And round in a ring swept the wild, wan rout,
Till the clock struck one—then each ghostly knave,
With a wailing howl, rush'd into his grave!

„Ich lag und schlief, und schlief recht mild."

 I FELL asleep, and quietly slept;
  Gone were my grief and care;
 In silent dreams before me swept
  A maid divinely fair.

 And pale as marble did she seem,
  And strangely gazed at me;
 Her eyes they had a pearly gleam,
  Her hair waved wondrously.

 And lightly in my vision pass'd
  That maiden pale and wan,
 And on my heart sank down at last
  That maiden pale and wan.

 How heaved and throbb'd with joy and woe
  The heart that burn'd in me!
 Nor heaved nor throbb'd her bosom so,
  But cold as ice was she.

'Nor heaves nor throbs with joy and woe
   This icy heart, yet well
The mighty power of love I know—
   Its heaven and its hell.

' Nor lips nor cheeks with roses shine,
   Nor red blood warms my heart;
Yet shudder not, for I am thine—
   My only love thou art!'

And wilder yet she clung to me,
   My heart grew chill with dread;
Then crow'd the cock, and silently
   The pale wan maiden fled.

„Da hab' ich viel' blaſſe Leichen."

THE ghastly spectres grieve me
   I summon'd by word of might;
They came, but will not leave me,
   To sink to their ancient night.

The spell that is their master
   I've forgotten, to my dismay;
To perdition, fast and faster,
   The spectres drag me away.

Down to where darkness gloometh!
   Begone!—nor drag me so,—
There's many a joy still bloometh
   That I in the world may know.

Fain would I struggle and strive for
    A flower I 've long watch'd o'er—
Ah, what is there left to live for,
    If I must love no more?

O once, but once, to fold her
    In my bosom, glowing and fain!
O once with kisses to hold her—
    Wild kisses of sweetest pain!

One kind, loving word, could I hear it—
    One whisper, my love, from thee—
I 'd follow that grisly spirit,
    And the darkest of destinies dree.

The listening ghosts draw near me,
    Their terrible nods I see;
Ah, darling, darling, hear me;
    Sweet love, ah, lov'st thou me?

SONGS.

„Morgens steh' ich auf und frage."

Up I start at morning, crying,
  'Will she come to-day?'
Down I sink at evening, sighing,
  'She is still away!'

Through the night my fate I ponder,
  Sad and sleepless aye;
Dreaming, half awake, I wander
  All the weary day.

„Ich wandelte unter den Bäumen."

O'erhead the leaves are shaking,
  Alone I wander in pain,
And the old dream awaking,
  Steals to my heart again.

Who taught you this word, ye birdies?
  Ah, cease your song in the tree!
My heart, when it hears this word, is
  Aweary and sad in me.

'"Twas here a maiden brought it;
  And ever she sang this word
So golden-sweet, she taught it
  To every listening bird.'

Sly birds, pray do not borrow
  Such stories to win me o'er;
Ye would wile away my sorrow,
  But I trust in no one more.

„Lieb Liebchen, leg'ß Händchen auf'ß Herze mein."

THY little hand lay on my heart, my fair!
Hear'st thou how it knocks in its chamber there?
There bides a carpenter—wicked is he,—
So busily making a coffin for me.

He knocks and hammers night and day,
And long has driven my sleep away:
Haste, Master Carpenter! haste, nor keep
Me longer awake—I fain would sleep.

„Berg' und Burgen schau'n herunter."

CLIFF and castle, downward glancing,
  In Rhine's silver bosom, see!
'Mid bright rings of sunshine dancing,
  Lo, my bark glides merrily.

While I watch the golden breaking
  Of the waves through which we dart,
Silently those thoughts are waking
  That lie deepest in the heart.

Gaily luring, kindly greeting,
  Gleaming, curls the dimpled flow;
While in light its breast is beating,
  Night and death lie hid below.

YOUTH'S SORROWS.

Bliss without, dark snares within thee,
    Stream, thou dost my love portray!
Nodding, as if friends thou 'dst win thee;
    Smiling sweetly—to betray.

„Anfangs wollt' ich fast verzagen."

First methought I 'd sink before it;
    Weary was my heart, I trow!
Nathless, you can see, I bore it—
    But pray do not ask me how.

„Mit Rosen, Cypressen, und Flittergold."

Fain would I deck this book of mine
As if it were a dear one's shrine,
With rose and cypress and gold-leaf gay,
And in it bury my songs away.

And would that I could this love entomb!
By the grave of love peace springs in bloom.
Folk pluck it there, but 'twill only be
In blossom on my grave for me.

Lo! here are the songs that once uprose
Wild as the lava in Etna's throes:
They leap'd from my inmost soul, and threw
Bright sparkling showers of fiery dew.

Now silent and death-like are they laid—
Cold, cold, and still as a misty shade;

Yet should the spirit of love pass o'er,
They'd kindle and sparkle as of yore.

And well I think 'twill yet be so:
Beneath love's spirit again they'll glow,
If ever this book shall reach thy hand,
Thou sweet love in yon distant land;

Then the spell shall be loosed that froze my lays,
And the sad, wan letters will upward gaze,
Ah, so imploring, in thine eye,
And whisper of love with many a sigh!

ROMANCES.

THE MOURNER.

Every heart is fill'd with sorrow
　For the pale youth, wrung with pain,
From whose brow no glad to-morrow
　Lifts the clouds of grief again.

Cooling breezes, pity laden,
　O'er his fever'd cheeks will play;
Many a coy and gentle maiden
　Fain would kiss his grief away.

In the greenwood see him wander,
　Far from noisy haunts of men;
Sweet the birds are warbling yonder,
　In their rustling leafy den.

But that joyous warbling dieth,
　Every bird sits hush'd and drear!
Mournfully the wildwood sigheth
　While the sad one draweth near.

THE MOUNTAIN VOICE.

Sadly adown the valley rode
　A trooper bold and brave;
'And do I go to my darling's arms,
　Or down to the darksome grave?'—
The mountain answer gave—
　'The darksome grave!'

And further then the trooper rode,
   A deep sigh heaved his breast:
'And do I go to the grave so young?
   Ah, well! in the grave is rest!'
The mountain voice confess'd—
   'The grave is rest.'

A tear roll'd down the trooper's cheek,
   A tear of bitter pain:
'And is rest for me in the grave alone?—
   Then for me the grave is gain!'
The voice made low refrain—
   'The grave is gain!'

THE TWO BROTHERS.

On the hill-top, silent, darkling,
   Stands the castle, wrapt in night;
Lights are in the valley sparkling,
   Swords are flashing wild and bright.

There the brothers, fierce and cruel,
   Rage and fight with bloody knife;
Say, what means this dreadful duel?
   Why this furious, raging strife?

Laura's eye shines bright and kindly—
   Countess Laura, sweet and fair,—
Both the brothers love her blindly—
   Thus it is they struggle there.

Which, then, does the maiden favour?
　　Which shall have her for his bride?
Ah, she keeps the secret ever!—
　　Out then, sabre, and decide.

Clash on clash rings down the valley,
　　Fiercer, wilder, grows the fight—
Ah, ye madmen! terrors sally
　　Grim and ghastly through the night.

Woe, ye brothers, blindly vying!
　　Woe, ah woe, thou bloody glade!
Each upon the sod is lying,
　　Slaughter'd by a brother's blade.

Many hundred years have flitted,
　　Many a race hath pass'd away,
And the castle, all unpitied,
　　Mutely crumbles to decay.

But at night strange forms of wonder
　　Gather in the gloomy glades;
Hush! 'tis midnight, and see yonder
　　Flash the brothers' eager blades.

SONG OF THE PRISONER.

My grannie bewitch'd poor Lizzie one day:
　　' Go, burn her!' folks 'gan to mutter;
But though the judge might scribble away,
　　No word of confession she 'd utter.

Loud shriek'd she 'Murder! O murder and woe!'
    When into a caldron they toss'd her;
But ere the reek could smother her, lo!
    To a raven she changed—and they lost her.

My black-wing'd grandmother, quickly flee
    From the dark clouds closing above me;
Through the bars of my dungeon come to me
    With cheese and cakes, an you love me.

My black-wing'd grandmother, hear my cries
    That I send to you in my sorrow—
Don't let old auntie pick out my eyes
    When I swing in a rope to-morrow.

THE GRENADIERS.

Two grenadiers, in Russia ta'en,
    To France were homeward faring,
But when they reach'd a German inn,
    They hung their heads despairing;

For there a woful tale hear they—
    France lost and all forsaken—
Vanquish'd and shatter'd her *grande armée*—
    And the Emperor, the Emperor taken!

The bitter tears bedim their eyes—
    Their hearts are fill'd with yearning:
'Ah me! what pain is this?' one cries;
    'How my old wound is burning!'

The other sighs : ' That play is done,
    And death with thee I 'd cherish ;
But ah ! my wife and little one,
    If I come not, will perish.'

' What care I for wife or child ?
    Far deeper longings waken :
Let them go beg with hunger wild—
    My Emperor, my Emperor taken !

' Grant me, my brother, this one prayer ;
    I 'm dying—don't gainsay me—
But carry me back to France, and there
    In kindly French earth lay me.

' My honour-cross, with its crimson band,
    Place thou on the heart that stirr'd me,
And clasp the gun in my clenchèd hand,
    And with my sabre gird me.

' Thus still will I bide among the dead,
    Like a sentinel, till the rattle
And roar of cannon shall thunder o'erhead,
    And the tramp of the steeds to battle.

' When rides my Emperor over my grave,—
    Swords' clank and glitter attending,—
Then, ready arm'd, I'll spring from the grave—
    The Emperor, the Emperor defending ! '

THE MESSAGE.

Up! up! good knave, go saddle thy steed;
　　In hot haste mount and hie
O'er hill and dale and wood, until
　　King Duncan's towers are nigh.

There in his stable wait, and when
　　The menial comes, then say—
'Which of King Duncan's daughters is 't
　　That's bonnie bride to-day?'

And should he say—'The dark one is!'
　　Then hither quickly come;
But should he say—'The fair one is!'
　　Ride not so swiftly home!

But go into the town, and buy
　　A rope to take with thee,
And slowly ride; speak not a word—
　　But bring that rope to me.

THE HOME-GOING.

I go not alone, my lady fair!
　　We two must wend together
To the dear old house, the home of my childhood
To the drear cold house, so lone in the wildwood—
My mother at the door will be
Watching and wearying for me.

O get thee hence, thou gloomy man!
    Who was 't bid thee hither?
Thine eyes flash fire, thy breath 's aglow,
Thy hand is ice, thy cheek is snow.
O leave me alone to sing and dance
Where roses bloom and sunbeams glance!

Let the roses bloom, let the sun shine bright,
    My sweet! my darling!
Around thee fling the bride's attire,
And sweep the strings of the sounding lyre—
A bridal song thou 'lt sing to me
While the night-wind pipes the melody.

DON RAMIRO.

'Donna Clara! Donna Clara!
Many long years loved and courted;
Thou hast doom'd me to my ruin,
Thou hast doom'd me without pity!

'Donna Clara! Donna Clara!
Life is sweet though life be cheerless;
Fears and horrors lie beneath us
In the cold grave, dark and gloomy.

'Donna Clara! 'tis to-morrow
That Fernando at the altar
As his happy bride will greet thee—
Wilt thou bid me to the wedding?'

'Don Ramiro! Don Ramiro!
Bitter are the words thou speakest;
Harsher than the stars above us,
Yonder, mocking my heart's wishes.

'Don Ramiro! Don Ramiro!
Shake away that gloomy sadness—
Some sweet maiden yet awaits thee;
But we two by God are parted.

'Don Ramiro! thou who bravely
Many a Moorish host hast conquer'd,
Conquer now thyself, Ramiro!—
Come to-morrow to my wedding.'

'Donna Clara! Donna Clara!
I will come! yes, hear me swear it!
In the dance with thee I'll foot it.
Sweet, good-night! I'll come to-morrow.

'Sweet, good-night!' The window rattled;
Sighing stood Ramiro under,
Pale and silent like a statue,
Then stole forth into the darkness.

And at last night long and dreary
Flies before the sunny dawning:
Like a brightly blooming garden
Lies Toledo, widely scatter'd.

Palaces and lordly mansions
Shimmer in the gleaming sunshine;
Lofty dome and tower and steeple
Bright as burnish'd gold are flashing.

Like the hum of bees a-swarming
Merry peals and chimes are tinkling;
While from holy house and cloister
Rise the grateful hymns of morning.

But see yonder, what commotion!
Slowly from the market chapel
Crowds are swarming, crowds are streaming,
Gay with flowers and gala-dresses.

Gallant knights and lovely ladies
And gay courtiers there are shining;
Joyous clash the bells above them,
And, between, the organ thunders.

Yet apart from all, with honour,
In the middle of the people,
Walk that young and gallant couple—
Donna Clara, Don Fernando.

To the palace of the bridegroom
Crowds the joyous throng of people;
There the wedding feast beginneth
Bravely, in the good old fashion.

Now with tournament and feasting,
Now with song and loud rejoicing,
Swift the merry hours speed onward,
Daylight fades and night approaches.

In the palace then they gather,
Sweeping round in merry dances,
And the bright hall shines and blazes,
And the festive garments glitter.

On a dais raised and lofty
Bride and bridegroom sit together—
Donna Clara, Don Fernando—
Sweetly there they chat and whisper.

And the dancers, sweeping, whirling,
Through the bright hall gleam and glitter;
And the loud drums beat and rattle,
And the trumpets clang and clamour.

'Wherefore, dear and lovely lady,
Dost thou gaze so rapt and silent
Tow'rds that distant corner yonder?'
Thus the bridegroom spake in wonder.

'Dost not see, then, Don Fernando,
Some one in a dark, black mantle?'
And the knight smiled kindly on her—
'Ah, 'tis but an empty shadow!'

Nearer, nearer drew the shadow—
And a man was 'neath the mantle;
Clara, blushing, quickly knew him—
'Twas Ramiro that she greeted.

Down the hall now, sweeping, sailing,
Fast and furious wheel the dancers,
Round in mad and giddy waltzes,
And the broad floor groans and quivers.

'Gladly will I, Don Ramiro,
Dance with thee, since thou hast ask'd me,
Yet I would thou hadst not come here
In that black and gloomy mantle.'

With fix'd, piercing eyes, Ramiro
Gazes on the lovely Clara,
Clasps her firm, and mutters darkly—
'Thou didst bid me to thy wedding!'

Through the maze and merry tumult
Wheel and sail the two together;
And the loud drums beat and rattle,
And the trumpets clang and clamour.

'Snow-white are thy cheeks, Ramiro!'
Whispers Clara, inly trembling;
'Thou didst bid me to thy wedding!'
Hollow mutters Don Ramiro.

In the hall the tapers flicker
As the crowd sweeps madly onward;
And the loud drums beat and rattle,
And the trumpets clang and clamour.

'Ice-cold are thy hands, Ramiro!'
Whispers Clara, fearful, shuddering;
'Thou didst bid me to thy wedding!'—
And they whirl among the dancers.

'Leave me! leave me! Don Ramiro,—
Cold and death-like is thy breathing;
But again the dark words thrill her—
'Thou didst bid me to thy wedding.'

'Neath the dance the floor is glowing,
Loud the merry music soundeth;
Like a wondrous magic-weaving,
All is madly whirl'd together.

SONGS AND LYRICS.

'Leave me, leave me, Don Ramiro!'
Whimpers Clara 'midst the dancers:
Don Ramiro answers ever—
'Thou didst bid me to thy wedding!'

'In the name of God, now leave me!'
Clara cries with firmer utterance;
And the words were hardly spoken
Ere Ramiro vanish'd from her.

Clara, pale and numb with horror,
Sinks, while blank cold night sweeps o'er her,
And a swoon bears her bright spirit
To its dark and gloomy kingdom.

But the clouds and darkness leave her,
And once more her eyes she opens;
Then with wonder and amazement
Closes them again, and trembles.

Since the dance began, she never
From the dais has arisen;
Still she sits beside the bridegroom,
Who with anxious eye beholds her.

'Speak! what means this ashy paleness?
Wherefore are thine eyes so troubled?'—
'And Ramiro!' stammers Clara,
Stricken dumb with fear and horror.

But with bended brow the bridegroom
Sternly thus replied unto her:—
'Lady, news of blood why ask for?—
Ere the noon pass'd, died Ramiro.'

BELSHAZZAR.

The midnight hour was drawing on ;
Still as the grave lay Babylon.

But in the palace of the king
Were noisy mirth and revelling.

There 'mid his peers and nobles all,
Belshazzar feasts in his banquet-hall.

His courtiers round him glitter and shine,
Draining beakers of sparkling wine.

They clink the beakers and shout aloud ;
And the king is haughty, the king is proud.

There's a flush on his cheeks, a fire in his eyes,
And daring thoughts in the wine-cup rise.

Above the revel his voice is heard,
And he curses God with an impious word.

He vaunts himself, and rails, and jeers,
And the hall resounds to the shouting peers.

The king looks round with a haughty eye ;
A servant hastens at his cry ;

Aloft the vessels of gold he brings,
Robb'd from the house of the King of kings.

Then grasps the king with impious grip
A sacred goblet fill'd to the lip.

He drains at a draught the goblet dry,
And with lips a-foam doth jeering cry :—

'Jehovah! I scorn Thee and Thy throne!—
I am the King of Babylon!'

But scarce had the fearful words been said,
Ere shook the heart of the king with dread;

The loud laugh died to a shrinking breath,
And all in the hall was still as death.

And lo! on the high wall, broad and bare,
The hand, as the hand of a man, was there;

And wrote, and wrote on the wall, in red,
Red letters of fire, and vanishèd.

The dumb king gazed with awe and affright,
His joints were loosen'd, his face was white;

Crept through the crowd an icy thrill,
None moved, and every lip was still.

The Magi came, yet vain were all
To read the writing on the wall;

But his courtiers rose that night with care,
And fell on the king and slew him there.

THE WOUNDED KNIGHT.

Sad in my heart is written
   A tale of the days of old—
A knight he lies love-smitten;
   His fair one is faithless and cold.

And now must he look upon her
  As false whom he loves so true;
Now deem it a dishonour
  That love should thrill him through.

Into the lists see him rattle,
  And wildly throw his glove—
'Let him be ready to battle
  Who dares to slander my love!'

But all are silent around him—
  All, save his own fierce pain;
And he turns his lance to wound him,
  And strikes his heart in twain.

THE VOYAGE.

I LEAN'D against the bending mast,
  And every billow counted;
Adieu, my lovely fatherland!
  And o'er the surge we mounted.

Her casement glitter'd as I pass'd,
  Sweet, how my heart was beating!
I almost gazed my eyes away;
  But no one waved a greeting.

O cease to flow, ye blinding tears,
  For sight undimm'd I languish;
And thou, poor heart! ah, do not break
  Beneath this weight of anguish!

THE SONG OF REPENTANCE.

Sir Ulrich rides through the forest glade,
    The leaves they rustle and glisten;
Betwixt the boughs he sees a maid,
    Who seems to stop and listen.

The young knight says: 'Ah, well I know
    That sweetest of sweet faces;
It haunts me still where'er I go
    In towns and desert places.

'Two dewy roses are the lips,
    So fresh and bright they glitter,
Yet from between them often slips
    A cruel word and bitter.

'That witching mouth that wounds and grieves,
    A rose-bush doth resemble,
Where wily snakes, among the leaves,
    With venom hiss and tremble.

'That lovely dimple in the cheek—
    That dimpled sweet so takes me,
It is the grave that I must seek—
    A frenzied yearning makes me.

'And yonder, round the fairest head,
    Glimmer the sunniest tresses—
That is the net the devil outspread,—
    Now close about me it presses.

'Yon clear blue eyes, whose liquid look
  Seems something more than mortal,
For the gate of heaven itself I took—
  Alas! 'twas hell's own portal.'

And further Sir Ulrich rode through the wood,
  Sad rustled the green leaves o'er him;
When, tearful and wan, at a distance stood
  Another vision before him.

The young knight spake: 'O mother mine!
  How yearn'd thy bosom toward me,—
How long I vex'd that heart of thine
  With the passionate thoughts that stirr'd me!

'O to dry thine eyes with this hot pain
  Of grief, that nought can smother!
O to redden thy thin wan cheeks again
  With my heart's blood, dearest mother!'

And further he rode through the darkling glade,
  As the daylight was a-dying;
Strange voices 'gan to stir in the shade,
  And the evening winds were sighing.

The young knight listens, and hears his words,
  And deems the echoes flout him;
'Tis only the happy little birds
  That warble all about him—

'A charming song Sir Ulrich sings,
  The song of a heart that rueth;
And when to an end his chant he brings,
  That strain he aye reneweth.'

ON HEARING A LADY SING AN OLD BALLAD.

THAT lovely siren long will haunt me.
   I see her still, as on that day
When her sweet voice's soft appealing
Woke in my heart the deepest feeling,
While down my cheek the tear-drops stealing
   Told what no words of mine could say.

Dreams of long-vanish'd years came o'er me,—
   Methought I was a child again,
And by the lamp I well remember
Sat silent in my mother's chamber
To read old tales, while drear December
   Sobbed weirdly at the window-pane.

The tales with life began to quiver;
   The knights are rising from their graves;
To Roncesvalles to join the battle
Sir Roland rides, while round him rattle
Many keen swords, and that vile chattel
   Base Ganelon, the knave of knaves.

Betray'd by him is brave Sir Roland,
   He swims in blood and breathes with pain;
Scarce may his horn, though far he send it,
Reach Charlemagne; and all unfriended
The brave Sir Roland's days are ended—
   And with him dies my dream again.

A long and loud confusèd echo
   Brought back to me the common day;

The song had ceased, my dreams were routed
By folk who clapp'd their hands, and shouted
'Bravo!' with emphasis undoubted.—
　The singer bow'd and moved away.

THE SONG OF THE DUCATS.

Golden ducats, once my own,
Tell me, whither have ye flown?

Are ye with the golden fishes,
That where sunny waters shimmer
Leap and dive i' the joyous glimmer?

Are ye with the golden flowerets,
That in meadow green lie netted,
And with pearly dews are fretted?

Are ye with the golden songsters,
That in joy are upward driven
To the shining blue of heaven?

Are ye with the golden starlets,
That all night in troops of glory
Smile in heaven their radiant story?

Ye, my pretty golden ducats,
Swim not through the waves in light,
　Sparkle not with pearly dew,
　Fly not toward the shining blue,
Smile not in the heavens all night—
But the duns I plagued so much
Hold ye with a greedy clutch.

DIALOGUE ON PADERBORN HEATH.

Hear'st thou not these strains of wonder,
    Double-bass and fiddle sounding?
Many a maiden dances yonder,
    O'er the greensward gaily bounding.

'Ah, my friend, 'tis stuff you're speaking,
    There's no music far or near now;
Only little piggy's squeaking
    And the old one's grunt I hear now.'

Hear'st thou not the bugle playing?
    Huntsmen through the greenwood hie them
Yonder gentle lambs are straying,
    And the shepherd piping by them.

'Ah, my friend, I hear no blaring—
    Neither horns nor pipes awaken;
'Tis the sow-herd homeward faring
    With his porkers—you're mistaken.'

Hear'st thou float through air's dominions
    Strains as minstrels sweet were vying?
Gladden'd angels strike their pinions
    When such strains are upward sighing.

'Ah, the music that so pretty
    From the distance seems to wander,
Is the younker's lively ditty
    Homeward driving goose and gander.'

Hear'st thou not from village steeple
  Sweet bells sounding down the valley?
To the church good pious people
  Wend by field and shady alley.

'Ah, that is the tinkling rattle
  Of the cow-bells, gently shaking,
As with drooping heads the cattle
  For their stalls are slowly making.'

See'st thou not that mantle streaming?
  See'st thou not that kindly greeting?
There I see the dear one beaming!—
  Tearful are thine eyes, my sweeting!

'Ah, my friend, no fair one noddeth;
  There I see no bright nonesuches—
Only cripple Bess who ploddeth,
  Pale and haggard, on her crutches.'

Now I see thee stare with wonder,
  Stifled laughter in thy glances—
What my bosom labours under,
  Dost thou take for idle fancies?

QUITE TRUE.

When spring-time comes with its sunny sheen,
  Then the flowerets wake from their winter sleep;
  When the moon begins through the sky to sweep
Then follow the stars their radiant queen.

When the poet two beautiful eyes doth see,
Then songs from his inmost heart sings he:—
But songs and stars, and flowers and eyes,
And the sheen of the moon and sunny skies,
However delightful these may be—
They're a long way from making the world, d'you see?

LYRICAL INTERMEZZO.

PROLOGUE.

There once was a knight, wan and thin was his cheek,
   And grief mark'd every feature;
He totter'd and dawdled, aimless and weak,
   In a maze—for to dream was his nature.
So awkward, so clumsy, and absent was he,
The flowerets and maidens would titter to see
   The shuffling and stumbling creature.

At home oft he sat in the darkest nook,
   From every intruder concealing,
There stretch'd out his arm with a yearning look—
   A look of speechless appealing.
But when the midnight hour came round,
He heard a singing and tinkling sound,
   And a knocking—his loved one revealing.

There, robed in the lightsomest foam of the sea,
   To his feet a fair nymph advances;
And bright and sweet as a rose is she—
   Her jewell'd veil flutters and glances.
Round her form, light and slender, the golden locks shine,
And fondly they gaze, and warmly entwine,
   Deep drown'd in love's rosiest trances.

Thus close to his bosom the fair one he takes,—
  New fire in the mazed dullard gloweth;
The pale one flushes, the dreamer awakes,
  And bolder and bolder he groweth.
But she—she saucily plagues him the while,
And over his head, with a roguish smile,
  Her jewell'd veil cunningly throweth.

Then sudden the knight is ta'en by the sleight
  Of that nixie, graceful and slender,
To a water-palace so wondrous bright
  His eyes grow dim with the splendour.
Yet holds she her captive clasp'd to her side,—
The knight is bridegroom, the nixie is bride,—
  Her nymphs with music attend her.

So sweetly they play, and so sweetly they trill,
  Their feet in the dance lightly beating,
The knight is fast losing his senses, and still
  More tightly he clings to his sweeting.
When sudden the lights go out—and, see!
Alone in his poet's dark chamber sits he,
  And all his bright visions are fleeting.

„Im wunderschönen Monat Mai."

'Twas in the glorious month of May,
  When buds from sleep are breaking,
That warm within my bosom
  I felt love's first awaking.

'Twas in the glorious month of May,
    When birds' sweet notes are thronging,
That first to her I whisper'd
    My yearning and my longing.

„Aus meinen Thränen sprießen."

FLOWERS from my tears are springing,
    There many a bloom exhales;
And my soft sighs become, love,
    A choir of nightingales.

And if thou lov'st me, darling,
    All the flowers to thee I'll bring,
And sweet before thy window
    The nightingale's song shall ring.

„Die Rose, die Lilje, die Taube, die Sonne."

THE rose, the lily, the dove, the sun,—
I loved them all in the days that are done;
But now I love only a dear little fair one—
A sweet one, a neat one, a pure one, a rare one!
Sole fountain and source of love for me—
Rose, lily, and dove, and sun is she!

„Wenn ich in deine Augen seh'."

WHEN I look into thine eyes,
    Every pain and sorrow flies;

When I kiss thy budding lip,
There new lease of life I sip.

Leaning on thy breast divine,
What are angels' joys to mine!
But when thou sayest, 'I love thee!'
Then my tears fall bitterly.

„Dein Angesicht, so lieb und schön."

In dreams methinks I see thy face,
So full of love and gentle grace;
So like an angel's, meekly borne,
And yet so weary, wan, and worn.

Still on thy lips the roses play—
Death soon will kiss their bloom away:
Thine eyes that shed a heavenly light
Are darkening into endless night.

„Ich will meine Seele tauchen."

In the dainty cup of the lily
   I'll steep this spirit of mine,
And the lily shall tinkle shrilly
   A song of my love divine.

And the song it rings shall shiver
   And tremble like that kiss
When her lips to mine did quiver
   In a strange, sweet hour of bliss.

„Es stehen unbeweglich."

ALL through the ages shine they,
   Yon stars in heaven above;
And gaze upon each other
   With sad and yearning love.

They speak a wondrous language,
   Wealthy and sweet, no doubt;
Yet none of all our sages
   Its meaning can make out.

But I can—and shall never
   That meaning cease to trace.—
The grammar that assists me
   Is my beloved's face.

„Auf Flügeln des Gesanges."

AWAY! away! with me, love!
   On the wings of song we go;
Where Ganges wanders free, love,
   A beautiful spot I know.

Red, rosy blooms are shining
   In the moonlight still and fair;
And the lotus-flowers are pining
   For their little sister there.

The violets whisper and titter,
   And gaze at the stars above;
And the roses, sighing, twitter
   Their balmy tales of love.

The gazelle skips nigh to listen
   As the beautiful prattlers dream,
While in the distance glisten
   The waves of the sacred stream.

There, sweet! shall we, reclining
   Where the broad palm droops its crest,
Our souls to love resigning,
   Dream blissful dreams, and rest.

„Die Lotosblume ängstigt."

THE lotus-flower a-weary
   Of the sun's meridian light,
Droop'd its head in slumber,
   To dream of the coming night.

The moon, her lover, wakes her,
   With calm and tender rays,
And to him unveiling gladly
   She lifts her gentle face.

She blooms, and glows, and brightens,
   And gazes in silence above:
She sighs, and weeps, and trembles
   With the bliss and the pain of love.

„Du liebst mich nicht, du liebst mich nicht."

THOU lov'st me not, thou lov'st me not—
   But that shall ne'er distress me!
I look into thy face, and lo!
   What kingly joys possess me!

Thou hatest, yes, thou hatest me!—
    Thy rosy lips declare it;—
Pray, let me kiss them, little one,
    And so methinks I'll bear it.

„O schwöre nicht und küsse nur."

O SWEAR not! only kiss and kiss -
A woman's word ne'er trusted is;
Thy word is sweet, but sweeter be
The kisses I have ta'en from thee.
On these alone I rest my faith—
A word is but an idle breath.

    *   *   *

O swear, my darling, ever swear!
I trust thee in each word I hear!
Upon thy bosom I recline
And think my bliss indeed divine.
For ever, love! thou lovest me—
For ever?—nay, 'twill longer be!

„Auf meiner Herzliebsten Äugelein."

UPON thine eyes, beloved mine,
    I write most beautiful lyrics;
Upon that little mouth of thine
    I write the best terzinas:
Upon thy cheeks so fresh and fine
    I write the noblest stanzas;
And hadst thou but a heart, upon it
I'd write the most delicious sonnet.

„Liebste, sollst mir heute sagen."

LITTLE darling, tell me truly
   Is it some sweet dream thou art,
Such as golden summer duly
   Wakes within a poet's heart?

No! such lips, such eyes that quiver
   With a magic all their own—
Such a little darling never
   In a poet's dream was known.

Basilisks and monsters many,
   Vampires, dragons, hideous things,—
Such the fabled shapes uncanny
   That the dreaming poet sings.

Yes! but ne'er from poet's fancies
   Sprung thy perfidy and thee—
No! those false and tender glances
   Ne'er a poet's dream could be.

„Ich grolle nicht, und wenn das Herz auch bricht."

I'LL not reproach thee! though my heart should break,
Ever-lost love, I will no umbrage take.
Though with thy gems thou beamest fair and bright,
No beam illumes thy heart's dark, dreary night.

Long have I known it, and in dreams unblest
I saw thee and the night within thy breast:
I saw the serpent preying on thy heart;
I saw how wretched and how sad thou art!

LYRICAL INTERMEZZO.

„Ja du bist elend, und ich grolle nicht."

YES! thou art wretched, and no plaint I make;
  Dear love of mine, we both must wretched be!
Till death our worn and weary hearts shall break,
  Dear love of mine, we both must wretched be!

I see the scorn about thy lips that dwells,
  I see thine eyes, love, flash defiantly;
I see the pride with which thy bosom swells,—
  Yet thou art wretched—wretched, love, as I!

About thy lips lurk hidden grief and pain;
  Thine eyes are dim with tears thou'dst hide from me;
In thy proud bosom secret wounds remain;
  Dear love of mine, we both must wretched be!

„Das ist ein Flöten und Geigen."

THERE merry music soundeth,
  Flutes, fiddles, and trumpets play:
Through joyous circles boundeth
  My love on her wedding-day.

The pipe with the drum is vying,
  There's tinkle and clash and drone;
Meanwhile good angels are sighing
  With many a sob and moan.

„So hast du ganz und gar vergessen."

AND hast thou then forgotten fully
How long I held thy heart and truly?—
That heart so little and false and sweet—
A sweeter and falser never shall beat.

Are the love and woe forgot for ever,
That made my bosom throb and quiver?
Ah, which was greatest I cannot tell!
That both were great, I know too well.

„Und wüßten's die Blumen, die kleinen."

AND if each little blossom
   My heart's wound only knew,
Those flowers would weep, my bosom,
   Weep tears of balm for you.

And were the griefs that haunt me
   Known where the warblers stray,
The nightingales would chaunt me
   A soft and soothing lay.

And were the secret given,
   Yon golden stars would flee
Their radiant home in heaven
   To whisper hope to me.

From star and bird and blossom
   'Tis hid!—one only knows;
'Tis She hath rent my bosom,
   And caused me all my woes.

„Warum sind denn die Rosen so blaß."

WHY are the roses so wan and pale?
   O say, my darling, say!
Why are the violets of the dale
   So dumb in the grass to-day?

Why, dearest, does the lark repeat
   So tristful a song o'erhead?
Why breathes the wild thyme, once so sweet,
   Dank odours of the dead?

And why from the sun in heaven above
   Has all the brightness gone?
Why seems the earth like a grave, my love,
   So desolate and wan?

And why am I sad and sick at heart?
   Why, loved one, should this be?—
O why, heart's darling as thou art,
   Hast thou forsaken me?

„Sie haben dir Viel erzählet."

They've plain'd to thee and lamented,
   Thou'st heard their ceaseless chat;
But how my soul was tormented,—
   They could not tell thee that.

Much fuss would they make, and snivel
   Lugubrious, shaking the head;
They call'd me—yes, call'd me the devil—
   And thou didst believe what they said.

And yet, I know, the saddest
   And worst ne'er came to the day,—
The saddest and the maddest
   I hid in my heart away.

„Die Linde blühte, die Nachtigall sang."

THE linden blossom'd, the nightingale sung,
    The sun with joy the green earth caress'd;
You kiss'd me then, round my neck you hung,
    And drew me close to your throbbing breast.

The leaves were falling, the raven croak'd nigh,
    The sun blink'd sulkily over the lea,
Then coldly we bade each other 'Good-bye,'
    And a courtly courtsey you made to me.

„Die Erde war so lange geizig."

THE earth had been long a niggard of beauty
    Till prodigal May came to cheer up creation;
Now every one laughs and shouts as in duty,
    But as for myself I have no inclination.

The flowerets are blooming, the little bells tinkling,
    The birds talk in earnest and sweet conversation;
And yet of their meaning I have not an inkling—
    All's wretched about me, and that's my persuasion.

Now every one bores me—each son of old Adam—
    Yes, even my friends are a sore botheration;
And all this has come with that title of 'Madam'
    They've gi'en to my darling, to my consternation.

„Die blauen Veilchen der Äugelein."

HER eyes are violet, wet with dew,
Her cheeks are roses of dazzling hue,
Her hands are lilies fair to view,—
Bright and blooming as ever are they—
'Tis only her heart that has wither'd away.

„Die Welt ist so schön und der Himmel so blau."

THE world is fair and the heavens are blue,
And gently the zephyrs flutter and woo,
And the flowers peep up in the grass anew,
And glitter and shine in the morning dew,
And men are shouting—a joyful crew!
Yet would I were in the grave at rest,
With my dead love folded into my breast.

„Mein süßes Lieb, wenn du im Grab."

MY love, when thou art gone away,
   And the gruesome grave doth hold thee,
I 'll sink to thee from the joyless day,
   And in mine arms will fold thee.

I 'll kiss thee wan and cold in thy sleep,
   And wildly I 'll cling to my sweeting!
I 'll shout, I 'll tremble, gently I 'll weep
   Till my heart like thine cease beating!

The dead will rise at the midnight hour—
   They 'll dance—a shadowy number—
But we two will rest in our darksome bower,
   And pale on thy bosom I 'll slumber.

The dead will rise when the day of doom
    Shall bliss and woe deliver—
What's that to us? we'll bide in the tomb,
    Lock'd in our arms for ever!

„Ein Fichtenbaum steht einsam."

In the North a pine stands lonely
    On a mountain bleak and bare,
And wrapt in a snowy mantle
    It sleepeth and dreameth there.

It dreameth of a palm-tree,
    Which, all alone and still,
In the distant East stands mourning,
    On a parch'd and burning hill.

„Ach, wenn ich nur der Schemel wär'."

(The Head says :—)

Ah, were I but the stool so light
    Beneath the darling's foot divine,
Then let her press with all her might,
    A word of plaint should ne'er be mine.

(The Heart says :—)

Ah, were I but that cushion now
    In which her pins and needles be,
Whene'er she prick'd me sharp, I vow
    'Twould be a very joy to me.

LYRICAL INTERMEZZO.

(*The Song says:—*)

Ah, were I but the paper roll
  Round which a dainty curl she wreathes,
I'd whisper to her all the soul
  That in me ever lives and breathes.

„Seit die Liebſte war entfernt."

SINCE my loved one went afar
Smile and laugh forgotten are;
Folk may show their sorry wit,
But I cannot laugh at it.

Since I lost my love, no more
Weep I as I wept before;
Though my heart breaks with its woe,
Yet my tears no longer flow.

„Aus meinen großen Schmerzen."

THE little songs I utter
  Out of my griefs are fashion'd,
  They wave their wings impassion'd;
And light to her bosom they flutter.

And now to my love they have floated,
  Yet come they back appealing,
  Complaining, but never revealing
What they in her bosom noted.

„Philister in Sonntagsröcklein."

The cits in their Sunday dresses
  Ramble through field and wood,
They greet fair Nature that blesses,
  And frolic in lightsome mood.

They strive, with wide eyes blinking,
  Earth's fairy-like bloom to win,
And with long ears stand drinking
  The chirp of the sparrow in.

But I with dark cloth cover
  My chamber window alway,
And the spectres in darkness that hover,
  They visit me even by day.

And my old love upsweepeth
  From where all dead things be,
And sitteth beside me, and weepeth,
  And melteth my heart in me.

„Manch Bild vergeßener Zeiten."

Dreams of old times forgotten
  Rise from their darksome bed,
And show while I was near thee
  The dreary life I led.

By day I stagger'd, dreaming,
  Through the city's busy hum,
And people gazed and wonder'd,
  So sad was I and dumb.

At night, I trow, 'twas better,—
  The din of life was gone,
And I with my shadow wander'd
  In silence and alone.

As o'er the bridge I sped me
  My footfall echoed loud;
The moon with a solemn greeting
  Peer'd through her dusky shroud.

Before thy house I linger'd,
  And long I gazed on high,
Gazed fondly at thy window;—
  O sick at heart was I!

I know from that window often
  Those callous eyes of thine
Have seen me stand like a statue
  Still in the wan moonshine.

„Ein Jüngling liebt ein Mädchen."

A YOUTH he loved a maiden,
  The maiden another chose,
But that one loves another,
  And with her to the altar goes.

The luckless maiden cannot
  The disappointment bear,
And weds the first that offers—
  The youth is in despair.

It is an old, old story,
    And yet 'tis ever new—
And he whose fate it pictures,
    His heart is rent in two.

„Hör' ich die Liedchen klingen."

When the song she sang so sweetly
    I hear as I heard at first,
Wild yearnings unman me completely,
    I feel as my heart would burst.

I seek the gloomy forest,
    Impell'd by despair and fears;
There, when my grief is sorest,
    It loses itself in tears.

„Mir träumte von einem Königskind."

I dreamt of a wan and tearful face,
    Of a king's child, fair as a flower,
And warm and lovingly did we embrace,
    In the greening linden bower.

'I do not wish thy father's throne,
    Nor crown nor sceptre sigh for,—
Of all his treasures, thee alone,
    Thou beautiful one, I die for!'

'That cannot be,' she said to me;
    'I lie where the cold worm turneth,
And only at night can I come to thee,
    For whom my bosom yearneth.'

„Mein Liebchen, wir saßen beisammen."

    In a little skiff I rested,
      O heart's delight, with thee,
    And calm was the night we breasted
      The swell of the boundless sea.

    The beautiful isle Enchanted
      Shone dim as the moonshine glanced;
    Thence fairy-like music panted,
      And gossamer cloudlets danced.

    And the bright mists waved and shifted,
      And sweeter the music grew;
    But we pass'd, and wearily drifted
      Away o'er the trackless blue.

„Aus alten Märchen winkt es."

    From olden legends springing
      There waves a snow-white hand,
    I list to the ringing and singing
      Of some bright magic land,

    Where mighty flowers are shining
      'Neath a golden even-sky,
    And gazing there and pining
      For love of their sisters nigh;

    Where the trees, a chorus making,
      With music fill the air;
    And dancing springs are breaking
      Into melody rich and rare;

And love-songs sweet are thronging —
   Ne'er heardst thou such a strain!
Till wondrous, blissful longing
   Cheats the sad heart of pain.

O that I could for ever
   Dwell in these realms of joy,
Where weariness comes never,
   And no dark cares annoy.

Often in dreams Elysian
   Through that bright land I stray,
But morning breaks — and the vision
   Fades like a mist away.

„Am leuchtenden Sommermorgen."

ON a sunny summer morning
   In a garden fair am I,
The flowerets whisper and prattle,
   But I pass silent by.

The flowerets whisper and prattle,
   And me with pity scan, —
'Be not unkind to our sister,
   Thou pale-faced, mournful man.'

„Es leuchtet meine Liebe."

IN its dim mysterious glory
   My love, you may perceive,
Is like a sad old story
   That's sung on a summer's eve:—

'In a garden fair, enchanted,
    Two lovers sigh'd in dreams;
There the nightingale's bosom panted,
    And glimmer'd the pale moonbeams.

'Still stands the maiden; her lover
    Does homage on his knees;
A giant springs from his cover—
    The maiden in terror flees.

'To earth the knight sinks, dying,
    The giant reels to his den—'
When I in my grave am lying,
    That tale will be ended then.

„Sie haben mich gequälet."

They worried me, and drove me
    Into a doleful state—
Some with their love—confound them!
    And others with their hate.

My very glass they drugg'd it,
    They poison'd the bread I ate—
Some with their love—confound them!
    And others with their hate.

But she who more than these others
    Has all but driven me mad—
For me no hate has cherish'd
    Nor a thought of love ever had.

„Es liegt der heiße Sommer."

WARM summer, love, is lying
    Upon that cheek so fair;
But in thy heart cold winter—
    Cold winter, love, is there.

Yet soon a change is coming,
    O thou my love that art;
With winter on thy cheeks, love,
    And summer in thy heart.

„Wenn Zwei von einander scheiden."

WHEN dearest friends are parting,
    Lock'd hand in hand are they;
With sighing and with weeping
    They tear themselves away.

We wept not as we parted;
    We sighed not 'Ah!' and 'Oh!'—
The weeping and the sighing
    Came afterwards, you know.

„Sie saßen und tranken am Theetisch."

AT the tea-table love was the topic,
    With this the gentlemen dealt
In a manner most philosophic;
    The ladies spoke as they felt.

'Love ought to be platonical!'
    The wither'd old Councillor cried;
His wife, with a smile ironical,
    A long-drawn 'Ah!' replied.

'Love should not be wild and unruly,'
    Said the big-mouth'd Canon, 'or, lo!
'Twill act on the health unduly;'
    The young lady lisp'd— 'How so?'

The Countess her deep feeling vented—
    'Love is a passion!' she cried,
And her cup with grace presented
    To the Baron at her side.

The company wanted completeness;
    My love, you should have been there:
You can with so much sweetness
    The tale of your love declare.

„Vergiftet meine Lieder."

AND if my songs are poison'd,
    What wonder it should be!
Thou hast, ah cruel! blighted
    The bloom of life for me.

And if my songs are poison'd,
    What wonder it should be!
In my heart are many vipers,
    And thee, my love, and thee.

„Mir träumte wieder der alte Traum."

I DREAMED again the same old dream,
  'Twas on a night in May;
We pledged our troth 'neath the linden-trees,
  And vow'd to keep it for aye.

We pledged it over and over again,
  With billing and cooing and petting;
And you bit my hand, that for me at least
  There should be no forgetting.

O darling, with the sweet clear eyes!
  O darling, love-inviting!
Although the vows were well enough—
  I could have spared the biting.

„Ich hab' im Traum geweinet."

IN dreams I fell a-weeping:
  Methought that thou wert dead;
I waked, and in the darkness
  Full many a tear I shed.

In dreams I fell a-weeping:
  Thou hadst forsaken me;
I waked, and long I wept, love—
  O long and bitterly!

In dreams I fell a-weeping,
  Methought thou still wert true;
I waked, sweet one! yet ever
  The tears my cheeks bedew.

„Allnächtlich im Traume seh' ich dich."

In the dreams of night I see thee,
   Ah, kindly dost thou greet!
I speak not, but in sorrow
   Fall weeping at thy feet.

Sadly thou lookest on me,
   Slow moves thy gentle head,
While, from thy bright eyes stealing,
   The pearly tears are shed.

A tender word thou leavest,
   And a cypress wreath, dear one!
I wake—ah, where is the wreath, love?
   And the whisper'd word is gone.

„Das ist ein Brausen und Heulen."

Wild is the night and eerie
   With tempest roar and moan;
Where lingers, sad and weary,
   My anxious little one?

At the window she is kneeling
   In her lonely little room;
From her eyes the tears are stealing,
   As she peers into the gloom.

„Der Herbstwind rüttelt die Bäume."

The trees in the autumn wind rustle,
   The night is damp and shrewd;
Close wrapp'd in my grey mantle,
   I ride alone through the wood.

My thoughts as I am riding
   Go running on before,
And airily they bear me
   To my beloved's door.

Loud bark the dogs; the servants
   In their hands bright torches bear;
My iron spurs ring loudly
   As I climb the winding stair.

In a sweet and cosie chamber,
   And bright with all her charms,
My darling one awaits me—
   I rush into her arms.

The wind through the leaves is sighing,
   And an old oak says to me,—
' What meaning, foolish horseman,
   In thy foolish dream can be?'

„Es fällt ein Stern herunter."

A STAR falls in the darkness
   Down from its glittering height;
'Tis the star of love, I know it
   As it shoots across the night.

Showers of leaves and blossoms
   Fall from the apple-trees,
To and fro they flutter,
   And dance with the wanton breeze.

On the mere the swan sings softly
    As it gently breasts the wave,
Till, faint and fainter singing,
    It sinks to its oozy grave.

The night is dark and stilly,
    The blooms and leaves are gone,
The star to dust has crackled,
    And silent is the swan.

„Nacht lag auf meinem Augen."

NIGHT lay upon my eyelids,
    My lips were heavy and wan;
Benumb'd were brain and bosom;
    In the grave I slumber'd on.

How long I lay thus silent,
    With dreamless heart and head,
I cannot tell, when a knocking
    I heard in my darksome bed.

' Wilt thou not rise, my Henry?
    The endless day doth break,
And the dead, aroused from slumber,
    To eternal joys awake.'

' I cannot rise, my darling!
    For me there is no light:
My eyes with bitter weeping
    Are closed in endless night.'

'O, I will kiss them, Henry!
    Kiss night from thine eyes away;
And thou shalt see the angels
    Shining in lasting day.'

'I cannot rise, my darling!
    Deep in my bosom's core,
Where thy sharp word did stab me
    The blood flows evermore!'

'Upon thy bosom, Henry,
    My hand will I gently lay;
Then shall thy wound cease bleeding,
    And the pain shall pass away.

'I cannot rise, my darling!
    My head is bleeding free;
'Twas there I sent a bullet
    When thou wert rapt from me.'

'Then with my tresses, Henry,
    Will I wipe the bleeding pain,
And staunch the blood for ever,
    And make thee well again.'

Her voice so soft, so tender,
    Touches my bosom so,
Fain would I rise in the darkness,
    And to my darling go.

Then all my wounds burst open,
    And again doth wildly break
The blood from head and bosom;—
    And lo! I am awake!

„Die alten, bösen Lieder."

THE old songs, wild and wicked,
   The gruesome dreams, and all—
Let's bury them for ever;
   For a mighty chest I call.

I've much to hide within it—
   What must yet a secret be:
The Heidelberg great tun won't
   Be big enough for me.

And let a bier be brought me
   Of good thick planks and strong,
And see that they be longer
   Than the bridge at Mainz is long.

Fetch me also twelve great giants
   Of stronger thews and bone
Than Christopher the Holy
   In the Dome at Cologne.

They shall carry forth the coffin,
   And sink it in the wave;
For such a mighty coffin
   Demands a fitting grave.

Can you guess why the coffin
   Must so large and heavy be?—
My love and all my sorrow
   It shall bury in the sea.

THE RETURN HOME.

„In mein gar so dunkles Leben."

In my life so dark and dreary
   Beam'd a vision sweet and bright;
That sweet vision now has faded;
   Round me gather gloom and night.

Little children in the darkness
   Faint of heart and shrinking are;
Loud they sing a cheery ditty,
   Anxious thoughts to drive afar.

I, a foolish child, I sing me
   In the dark my little lay;
What although it be unpleasing—
   It has driven sad care away.

„Ich weiß nicht was soll es bedeuten."

I know not what sad fate befalls me,
   But heavy at heart am I;
An eerie legend enthralls me—
   A tale of the days gone by.

THE RETURN HOME.

The air is cool and darkling,
    Rhine softly steals away,
And the mountain-tops are sparkling
    In the flush of dying day.

Where the rocks in the red light shimmer,
    A beautiful maid sits there,
And bright her jewels glimmer
    As she combs her golden hair.

And her golden comb still glistens,
    While all the welkin rings;
And the dreaming boatman listens
    To the luring song she sings.

And the listener's heart is laden
    With yearning love and woe:
He gazes up at the maiden
    Nor thinks of the rocks below.

The wan waves have no pity,
    He sinks with the sinking sun—
And that with her eldritch ditty
    The Loreley has done.

„Mein Herz, mein Herz ist traurig."

SAD is my heart and weary,
    Yet lustily shines sweet May;
I lean against a linden
    On the bastion old and grey.

Below me, drowsily flowing,
   Is the still blue city moat,
Where a boy, fishing and whistling,
   Floats on in his little boat.

Dwarf'd in the distance yonder
   O'er many a dappled rood,
Are houses, and gardens, and people,
   And cattle, and meadows, and wood.

On the grass white clothes are bleaching,
   The maidens trip around,
And the mill-wheel scatters diamonds—
   I hear its distant sound.

Hard by the old grey tower
   Is the sentry's shelter-place;
And to and fro in his red coat
   I see that sentry pace.

He plays with his polish'd firelock,
   Which glints in the sunshine red—
He shoulders it and presents it;
   I wish he would shoot me dead.

„Im Walde wandl' ich und weine."

SAD through the wood I wander,
   The throstle sits high on a bough
And flutters her wings, singing yonder—
   'O why so woful art thou?'

Could the swallows, thy sisters, confess all,
  'Tis they could tell thee why:—
In cunning retreats they nestle
  My darling's window by.

„Wir faßen am Fischerhauſe."

WE sat by the fisherman's cottage
  And gazed across the sea,
The mists of eve around us
  Were rising silently.

The lamps within the lighthouse
  Were lit up one by one,
And far away in the distance
  A ship lay all alone.

We talked of storm and shipwreck;
  Of the hardy sailor-boy,
Toss'd between sea and heaven,
  Anxiety and joy.

Of far-off foreign countries,
  Of North and South we spoke,
Discussing the strange manners
  And customs of strange folk.

By the Ganges are sweetness and brightness
  And giant-blooming bowers,
Where kneel in silence fair mortals
  Before the lotus-flowers.

In Lapland are dirty people,
    Flat-pated, broad-mouthed, and small;
They cower round the fire, baking fishes,
    And chatter, and screech, and squall.

Eager the maidens listen'd;
    At last we spoke no more:
The ship was gone, and darkness
    Rested on sea and shore.

„Du schönes Fischermädchen."

THOU pretty fisher-maiden,
    Row in thy boat to land,
And sit thee down beside me,—
    We'll prattle hand in hand.

Thy head lean on my bosom,
    And have no doubt of me—
Dost thou not daily trust thee,
    All fearless, to the sea?

My bosom, like the ocean,
    Has storm, and ebb, and flow;
And many pearls of beauty
    Sleep in its depths below.

„Der Sturm spielt auf zum Tanze."

THE storm plays weird dance music,
    It whistles and roars and howls:
Hurrah! how the little ship boundeth!
    The wild night bellows and scowls.

The sea in living mountains
   Heaves to the inky sky!
Here yawning in dark abysses,
   There breaking in foam on high.

And curses, and retching, and prayers
   Loud from the cabin come,
As fast to the mast I am clinging,
   And sighing—'I wish I were home.'

„Der Abend kommt gezogen."

THE clouds are creeping downward,
   Night comes with its doubts and fears;
'Mid the dark waves, rolling onward,
   A dim white form appears.

Nearer the mermaid, sweeping,
   Leaps from the breakers to me;
Over her thin vest peeping
   Breasts white as the snow can be.

She clings to me fast; she holds me,
   And much I fear her might:
Too fast thine arm enfolds me,
   Thou beautiful water-sprite.

'Thus wild are my caresses,
   For cold is the night to me;
And thus my bosom presses
   To share thy warmth with thee.'

The moon peers ever drearier
   Down from the dusky height;
Thine eye grows wet and wearier,
   Thou beautiful water-sprite.

'Not wet and weary it groweth;
   The tears that dim mine eyes,
The crispèd sea bestoweth
   When out of the waves I rise.'

Sad shrieks the mew as it fleeteth,
   Loud breaks the sea in its might:
Thy heart it wildly beateth,
   Thou beautiful water-sprite.

'My heart is wildly swelling
   For thee and for thy race,
With love that is past all telling,
   Thou kindly human-face.'

„Am fernen Horizonte."

Far on the dim horizon
   The city with its towers
Floats like a cloudy vision,
   While dark the twilight lowers.

A cold wet wind is blowing,
   And ruffles the water wan:
Monotonous and dreary
   Roweth the sailor on.

The sun a farewell gleameth
  From the rim of the level sea,
And lights up the far-off city
  Where my love was lost to me.

„Still ist die Nacht, es ruhen die Gassen."

'Tis night, not a sound through the streets doth go:
  And this was my darling's house, I wot;
She left the city a long time ago,
  But the house still stands in the self-same spot.

And there stands a man too, gazing on high,
  And wringing his hands in piteous case;
The moon shines out, and I shudder as I
  My own features see in his pinch'd wan face.

You double! you fellow with the pinch'd wan face,
  Why do you mimic the part I bore
In that sad love-tale, when I stood in that place
  Full many a night in the days of yore?

„Wie kannst du ruhig schlafen."

How canst thou sleep so quietly?
  Thou know'st I'm quite awake:
Should the old anger rouse me,
  My yoke I'd quickly break.

Hast the old song forgotten
  How once a clay-cold knave
At midnight snatch'd his sweetheart
  And bore her away to the grave?

Believe me, thou in beauty
    All maids surpassing far,
I live, and am much stronger
    Than all the dead folk are.

„Die Jungfrau schläft in der Kammer."

A MAIDEN slept in her chamber,
    The moon look'd tremulous in:
Without there was singing and tinkling,
    Like a dance's merry din.

' Now I will see from my window
    Who scares my sleep away ' :—
There stood a skeleton, fiddling,
    And singing the while to its play—

' Thou once to the dance didst tryst me,
    That tryst was broken by thee;
Now in the churchyard the dance is—
    Come there and freak with me!'

A spell is upon the maiden,
    It draws her away from the door;
She follows; the skeleton, singing
    And fiddling, strides before.

It fiddles, and skips, and hops there,
    And clatters with its bones;
And nods and nods its skull, while
    The moon shines down on the stones.

„Ich stand in dunkeln Träumen."

I stood in dark dreams gazing
  On a picture of my love;
Mysteriously the sweet face
  With life began to move.

About her lips played softly
  A tender, tremulous smile,
And tears as of weary yearning
  Glanced in her eyes the while.

My tears too flowed,—ah, darling,
  While fondly I look on thee,
I cannot quite believe yet
  That thou art lost to me!

„Die Jahre kommen und gehen."

The years are waxing and waning,
  And thousands go to the tomb,
But the flower of love in my bosom
  Still lives in immortal bloom.

O once again to meet thee,
  To fall upon my knee,
And, dying there, to whisper—
  'Madam, I love you—see!'

„Mir träumte: traurig schaute der Mond."

Methought that the moon shone mournfully,
  And sadly the stars were gleaming:
I was borne to the town where my loved one dwells,
  Many long leagues away, in my dreaming.

In silence I came to the step at her door,
   With kisses I tenderly press'd it;
There oft her garment has rustled past,
   And her little foot has rested.

Cold were the stones, the night was cold,
   And long it seem'd and dreary:
From the lattice look'd out in the pale moonlight
   A face that was wan and weary.

„Was will die einsame Thräne?"

WHAT means this lonely tear-drop
   That troubles thus mine eye?
'Tis the last surviving relic
   Of weary days gone by.

Its many shining sisters,
   Where are they?—vanish'd quite;
Gone with my joys and sorrows,
   Gone in the stormy night.

Gone too, like mist, for ever
   Are the little stars of blue,
That laugh'd into my bosom
   All the griefs and joys I knew.

Ah me! my love has faded
   Like dew at the dawn of day—
Thou last long-lingering tear drop,
   Do thou, too, fade away.

THE RETURN HOME.

„Der bleiche, herbſtliche Halbmond."

The sickle moon of autumn
   Glints pale the clouds between;
All lonely and still by the churchyard
   The pastor's house is seen.

The mother reads her Bible,
   The son at the lamp-light stares;
The elder daughter yawneth;
   The younger her weariness shares:—

'Ah, God!' she cries, 'time drowses;
   And long is the day to me:
Only when some one is buried
   Is there anything here to see!'

The mother looks up from her Bible:
   'You're wrong, for four have died
Since the day they buried your father
   By the churchyard gate outside.'

The elder daughter yawneth:—
   'I will not starve with you;
I'll go to the Count to-morrow—
   He is rich, and loves me too.'

The son bursts out a-laughing:—
   'At the "Star" drink huntsmen three,
Much money they make, and are willing
   To tell the secret to me!'

The mother throws her Bible
   Into his lean, lank face:
'And wouldst thou rob on the highway,
   Thou thrice-accurst and base?'

They hear a knock at the window,
   They see dark, beckoning hands;
There in his black priest-garments
   The pale dead father stands.

„Das ist ein schlechtes Wetter."

It rains, and snows, and blusters,
   The storm is at its height:
I sit at the window gazing
   Into the gloomy night.

Yonder a lone light twinkles,
   Slowly it moves abroad;
A mother with her lantern
   Totters across the road.

To buy flour, eggs, and butter,
   I'm sure the old body has come:
A cake she wishes to bake for
   Her big, plump daughter at home,

Where she at the light lies blinking,
   Half-asleep in her snug arm-chair—
Her rosy cheeks nigh hidden
   'Neath waves of golden hair.

„Man glaubt, daß ich mich gräme."

THEY tell me I am grieving
   And pining 'neath love's yoke,
Till now I almost credit
   The tale, like other folk.

Thou little one with the great eyes,
   I have vow'd to thee every day,
That my love is past all telling,
   That it gnaws my heart away.

But 'tis only alone in my chamber
   That I speak this way to thee:
For when I chance to be with thee
   I'm dumb as dumb can be.

Then wicked spirits plague me,
   They seal my lips, I trow;
And ah! 'tis through their malice
   That I'm so wretched now.

„Hat sie sich denn nie geäußert."

HAS she then no notice taken
   Of a love so warm and tender?
Could you in her eye discover
   No responsive sweet surrender?

Could not you by looks and glances
   Reach her heart, and so get at her?
Yet you once were thought no noodle,
   Worthy Sir, in such a matter!

„Sie liebten sich Beide, doch Keiner."

THEY both were in love, but neither
    The secret tale would betray:
Their looks were cold and unfriendly,
    Though with love they were pining away.

They parted at last for ever,
    And only in dreams they met:
They had long been dead, but hardly
    Was either aware of it yet.

„Und als ich euch meine Schmerzen geklagt."

WHEN I told you the sorrowful life I had led,
You yawn'd, but never a word you said;
But when I sung of it dainty-wise,
You praised my verses up to the skies.

„Ich rief den Teufel und er kam."

I CALL'D the devil and he came,
    And my eyes with wonder over him ran:
Neither ill-favour'd is he nor lame,
    But quite an agreeable, charming man,
In his prime, obliging, with plenty of tact—
A polish'd man of the world, in fact.
His diplomatic talent is great,
And he talks very well upon Church and State.
He's pale—but no wonder, for 'tis *en règle*
With him to study Sanscrit and Hegel;
His favourite poet is still Fouqué:

But with criticism he 'll no more bother;
  To Hecate, his dear grandmother,
He 's given that up for ever and aye.
My juridical studies he much commended:
To such studies he 'd once himself attended.
My friendship could not be, he vow'd,
Too dear to him—here he gracefully bow'd,
And ask'd if he had not met before
  At the Spanish Embassy with me?—
And when I look'd in his face once more,
  An old acquaintance he proved to be.

„Mein Kind, wir waren Kinder."

My little one, we were children,
  Our hearts were light and gay;
We crept into the hen-house,
  And hid below the hay.

Like fowls we crow'd and cackled
  And people, passing, heard—
Cock-a-doodle-doo! and fancied
  It was the very bird.

The boxes in the courtyard
  We paper'd well, and there
We dwelt, and thought our mansion
  Was grand beyond compare.

Oft came our neighbour's tabby
  To see us in our house,
And much respect we paid it,
  With compliments and bows.

'How do you, dear Pussic?
    Well?---Good!' we both exclaim;
Since then old cats a many
    Have heard us say the same.

And oft we sat and chatted
    Like grave old folk, and said,
'In our times things were better!'
    With a wise shake of the head.

'For love, and truth, and faith—all
    Have vanish'd from the earth!
And dear, too, is the coffee,—
    And money! what a dearth!'

Gone are our childish toyings,
    And everything, in sooth—
Old times, and the world, and money,
    And faith, and love, and truth.

„Das Herz ist mir bedrückt, und sehnlich."

My heart within me is a-weary,
    Musing upon the good old days;
Ah! then the world was bright and cheery,
    And folk still lived in quiet ways.

Now all that sweet, calm life has vanish'd;
    'Tis rush and crush for tear-stain'd bread;
God from His heaven above is banish'd,
    And down below the devil's dead.

Peevish and sad, of all bereft us,
  Our lives are canker'd, cold, inane;
But for the little love still left us,
  What rag of comfort would remain?

„Wie der Mond sich leuchtend dränget."

As yon moon in brightness breaketh
  Through the dusky clouds of night,
So to me through dark years shineth,
  Sweet and fair, a dream of light.

Crowds upon the deck were seated,
  Proudly Rhine swept on below,
And its banks, all green with summer,
  Shimmer'd in the even-glow.

Full of musings there I sat me,
  By a lady sweet as May;
In her face so fair, so pallid,
  Flash'd the ruddy golden ray.

Lutes were sounding, youths were singing,—
  Ah, what bliss entranced the whole!
Deeper grew the blue of heaven;
  Deeper, wider grew the soul.

Hill and castle, wood and meadow,
  Famed in story flitted by—
All their beauty saw I beaming
  In that lovely lady's eye.

„Herz, mein Herz, sei nicht beklommen."

HEART of mine, be not dejected!
   Let the years bring what they may;
Spring restores the long-expected
   Joys that Winter snatch'd away.

Heaven of all hath not bereft thee—
   Earth's bright beauty cannot pall;
What shall please thee?—this is left thee;—
   Thou dost live to love it all.

„Du bist wie eine Blume."

So fair, so pure, so gentle,
   Like some dear flower thou art;
I gaze on thee, and sadness
   Slides dumb into my heart.

I yearn, sweet one, to bless thee,
   To press thy sunny hair,
And pray God aye to keep thee,
   So gentle, pure, and fair.

„Wenn ich auf dem Lager liege."

WHEN on my couch I lay me,
   And pillow my weary head,
A dear and lovely vision
   Hovers around my bed.

And soon as the first kind slumbers
    Softly my eyelids kiss,
Then glides that lovely vision
    Into my dreams of bliss.

Yet with the dawn of morning
    It flitteth not away,
Deep in my inmost bosom
    I bear it all the day.

„Mädchen mit dem rothen Mündchen."

MAIDEN, with the lips so rosy,
    With the eyes so sweet and bright,
Thee, my darling little maiden,
    Thee I think of day and night.

Long is now the winter evening—
    Ah, to while away the hour,
Petting thee and chatting fondly
    In thy cosy little bower!

Little hand so white and dainty,
    Fain I'd kiss thee all the night!
Fain with tears would I caress thee,
    Little hand, so dainty-white.

„Verrieth mein blasses Angesicht."

CANST thou not read in my wan cheek
    The love 'neath which I languish?
And wouldst thou that these haughty lips
    'Sought thee to soothe mine anguish?

O these proud lips can only kiss,
  Or join in merry-making!
They might perhaps deride and scorn
  E'en while my heart was breaking.

„Theurer Freund, du bist verliebt."

WORTHY friend, thou art in love!
  Strange new pain thy patience taxes;
Darker grows it in thy head;
  Lighter in thy heart it waxes.

Worthy friend, thou art in love!—
  Don't attempt to hide thy yearning;
'Tis no use! thy heart's a-fire:
  Through thy vest I see it burning.

„Ich wollte bei dir weilen."

WHEN I with you would tarry,
  And set myself to woo,
Away you needs must hurry,
  You had so much to do.

And when, some short time after,
  I did my love avow,
You answer'd me with laughter,
  And a wicked mocking bow.

Yes, you severely tried me,
  My heart was sorely spent;
You know you even denied me
  A kiss before I went.

Don't think that I will scatter
   My brains out; for, you see,
This miserable matter
   Is nothing new to me.

„Saphire sind die Augen dein."

THINE eyes are sapphires, sweet and bright,
   Love in them shines and dances;
And oh! thrice happy is the man
   Who wins their loving glances!

Thy heart it is a diamond rare,
   A glorious light it gleameth:
And oh! thrice happy is the man
   For whom with love it beameth!

Thy lips are rubies—rubies red,
   Surpassing in their glory;
And oh! thrice happy is the man
   To whom they tell love's story!

O that I knew that happy man!
   O that, through greenwood wending,
I could but meet him all alone!—
   His luck should soon have ending.

„Ich wollt' meine Schmerzen ergössen."

IN one single word, could I utter
   The sum of my care and woe,
To the tricksy winds I would give it
   To carry wherever they go.

They should bear to thee, my darling,
    That sorrow-laden word;
And everywhere and always
    By thee it should be heard.

And even when in slumber
    Thine eyes had ceased to gleam,
My word should still pursue thee
    Into thy deepest dream.

„Du haſt Diamanten und Perlen."

DIAMONDS and pearls are thine, love!
    What heart but covets thy store?
And thou hast beautiful eyes, love!—
    My sweet, what wouldst thou more?

Full many immortal songs, love,
    Have I chanted o'er and o'er
In praise of thy beautiful eyes, love!—
    My sweet, what wouldst thou more?

With those beautiful eyes, my darling,
    Thou hast pierced me to the core,
And ruin'd me altogether—
    My sweet, what wouldst thou more?

„Gaben mir Rath und gute Lehren."

THEY counsell'd me, and well advised me,
Heap'd me with honours, said they prized me,
And if I'd only wait, I'd see
What wonderful things they'd do for me.

And yet I'm sure I should have perish'd
For all they did; but I was cherish'd
And help'd along by a good man,
Who proved a real Samaritan.

Ay, that he is!—I'll ne'er forget him!
He feeds me, and in my heart I set him!
'Tis pity he can't have a kiss from me—
But that good man is myself, you see!

„Habe auch in jungen Jahren."

How in youth love's glow hath brought me
Bitter pangs, and mischief wrought me,
    I could stories tell:
Now too costly is the fuel,
Faint and fail the flames so cruel—
    Ma foi! and that is well.

Pretty maiden, tears are silly,
Bid them go! and, willy-nilly,
    Banish foolish love's unrest.
Life's before thee—why regret it?
Leave the old love, and forget it,
    Ma foi! upon my breast.

„Auf den Wällen Salamanka's."

On the walls of Salamanca
    Fresh the breezes come and go,
There I wander with my donna
    In the summer even's glow!

And I clasp the slender beauty
   Of my loved and loving fair—
O how sweet to feel her bosom
   Heaving fond and proudly there!

Yet a strange, uneasy whisper
   Stealeth through the linden-tree,
And the mill-stream dark beneath us
   Murmurs evil dreams to me.

Ah, Senora! much I fear me,
   We shall never stray again
Here on Salamanca's ramparts—
   For they'll rusticate your swain.

„Wie dunkle Träume ftehen."

WHERE dreamlike stretch the houses
   In long and dark array,
My mantle wrapt around me,
   I take my silent way.

The tower of the Cathedral
   Clangs forth the midnight hour;
My sweet, with her charms and kisses,
   Awaits me in her bower.

The moon shines forth in glory,
   And lights me to my love;
I quickly reach her dwelling
   And joyful call above—

O moon, old friend, I thank thee
    That thou yon cloud hast furl'd,
Now leave me, I beseech thee,
    And cheer the rest of the world.

And shouldst thou find a lover
    Who all alone dost pine,
Be thou his best consoler,
    As thou hast oft been mine.

„Ach, die Augen sind es wieder."

AH, these are yet the very eyes
    Whose glances trembled through me;
And these are still the very lips
    That sweeten'd life unto me.

And this too is the same dear voice
    That once I heard so gladly;
I only am the same no more—
    Returned, but changed how sadly!

And now her lovely snow-white arms
    Are fondly round me stealing;
Wearied I lie upon her breast,
    Benumb'd in heart and feeling.

„Der Tod, das ist die kühle Nacht."

DEATH is the night, so cool, so calm,
    And life the restless, sultry day;
    Night comes, my eyes are heavy,
Of day so weary I am.

Over my bed there blossoms a tree
   Where pensive sings the nightingale;
   Her song of love ever warbles,
In dreams it comes to me.

„Sag, wo ist dein schönes Mädchen?"

Say, where is thy maiden sweet,
   Theme of all thy tender art?
Where the flames that once did beat
   Magic-mighty through thy heart?

Ah these flames no longer burn!
   Cold and sad at heart am I,
And this book is but the urn
   Where my dead love's ashes lie!

THE PILGRIMAGE TO KEVLAAR.

I.

At the window stands the mother,
   In bed her son doth lie:
'Wilt thou not rise, my William?
   The procession passes by.'

'O, weary am I and sick, mother,
   Nor hear can I nor see;
I think of my poor dead Gretchen,
   And sore is my heart in me.'

'Nay, rise! we will to Kevlaar
  With book and beads to-day;
So will the Blessed Mother
  Do all thy pain away.'

The sacred banners are waving,
  Sweetly the music flows;
To high Cologne on the river,
  There the procession goes.

With the crowd the mother keepeth,
  Her sick son leadeth she;
They sing together in chorus—
  'O Mary, praise to thee!'

II.

The Mother of God at Kevlaar
  Must don her best to-day;
With the sick will she be busy,
  Who come in crowds to pray.

The sick folk bring as offerings
  To the Holy Mother there
Limbs of the white wax fashion'd—
  Both feet and hands they bear.

And he who a wax hand offers
  Is heal'd where his own was sore:
And he who a wax foot offers
  Is lame in his own no more.

To Kevlaar went many on crutches,
    Now brisk on a rope dance they;
And fingers that late were helpless
    Now nimbly the viol play.

The mother brought a wax taper,
    And of it made a heart:
'Give that to the sweet God's Mother,
    So will she heal thy smart.'

And, sighing, the son brought the wax heart,
    And, sighing, knelt him there:
From his eye the sad tear trembled,
    From his heart went the woful prayer:

'O Thou for ever blessed!
    Pure maiden, holy one!
O lofty Queen of heaven!
    To thee my griefs be known!

'I dwelt with my old mother
    In Cologne, that city proud,
That city where in hundreds
    Chapels and churches crowd.

'And near us dwelt my Gretchen;
    Now she in her grave lies low:
Mary, I offer a wax heart—
    Heal thou my sick heart's woe.

'Heal my poor heart, and early
    And late my prayer will be—
My earnest hymn and prayer—
    "O Mary, praise to thee!"'

III.

The ailing son and his mother
    Sleep in their chamber, where
The Mother of God she cometh,
    And softly entereth there.

She bends her over the sick one,
    Her hand doth she tenderly lay
On his heart, and, smiling gently,
    Passes in silence away.

His mother sees all in her dreaming,
    And more, much more, sees she:
Then wakes she from her slumber,
    For the dogs bark furiously.

And there lay he outstretched—
    Her son, and he was dead:
On his wan cheek play'd lightly
    The morning golden red.

Her hands the mother folded,
    What mingled thoughts had she!
Resign'd, yet sang she softly,
    'O Mary, praise to thee!'

THE PRINCESS ILSE.[1]

I AM the Princess Ilse,
    And dwell in the Ilsenstein;
Come with me to my castle,
    Rare pleasures shall be thine!

[1] From the *Tour in the Harz*, 1824.

My crystal sparkling fountain
   I 'll sprinkle on thy brow,
And all thy pain will vanish,
   For sad at heart art thou.

Lock'd in my arms, and leaning
   Upon my snowy breast,
Thou 'lt dream of golden legends,
   And take thy happy rest.

I 'll fondle thee and kiss thee,
   As once, in days long fled,
I kiss'd and fondled Henry,
   The Kaiser, who is dead.

Only the live are living,
   The dead are dead for aye;
I still am fair and blooming,
   My heart beats ever gay.

Come to my sunken castle,
   Where all is crystal clear:
There dance brave knights and ladies,
   And squires shout o'er their cheer.

There rustle silken dresses,
   There spurs of iron ring;
There dwarfs sound drum and trumpet,
   And fiddle and pipe and sing.

But there my arms shall fold thee,
   Thou 'lt fare as the Kaiser fared:
I held him, and he heard not
   When loud the trumpet blared.

LATER POEMS.

NIGHT THOUGHTS.[1]

When, Germany, of thee I think
At night, I cannot sleep a wink,
But wide awake I lie and weary,
Weeping and musing, sad and dreary.

The years glide on with quickening pace:
Since last I saw my mother's face
Twelve years have gone, and fond thoughts thronging
Rouse all my yearning and my longing.

My yearning evermore doth grow,
That dear one has bewitch'd me so;
I think of her as of none other—
May God protect my dear old mother!

Deep is that mother's love for me,
And in her letters I can see
How tremulous her hand hath shaken,
As all her mother's heart did waken.

[1] This and the following four pieces are from the *Neue Gedichte* (New Poems), 1831.

Her shrine is in my bosom kept—
Twelve long, lone years have o'er me crept,
Twelve long, lone years since I caress'd her
And fondly to my bosom press'd her.

The fatherland doth ever stand,
It is a strong and healthy land;
Yon gleaming vale and shining river,
Yon oaks and lindens bide for ever.

But if my mother were not there,
For Germany I less should care:
Of fatherland you can't bereave me—
My mother, she may die and leave me.

Since from my native land I hied,
A many there I loved have died;
And while I reckon up the number
What grief is mine, what cark and cumber!

Yet must I count them all, and woe
Still wilder to my heart doth go.
I feel as though the dead lean'd o'er me!
Thank God, I wake—to see before me

My chamber-window gleam and glance
With thy bright sun, dear, joyous France!
And, look! my sweet French wife comes to me,
And doth from all these yearnings woo me.

„Es war ein alter König."

THERE was a king, an old king—
   His heart was sad, his hair was grey;
This poor old king he married
   A young bride, sweet as May.

There was a page, a young page,
   And light his heart, and bright his hair;
The youthful queen he tendeth,
   Her silken train to bear.

And dost thou know the old song,
   So sweet its sigh, so sad its sigh?—
Ah me! they love too kindly;
   They love, and they must die.

„Die blauen Frühlingsaugen."

Now spring's blue eyes are peeping
   O'er all the grassy lea,
Dear violets are opening
   And gazing up at me.

I pluck them, musing fondly,
   And every thought that plays
About my heart in secret
   The nightingale betrays.

Ah yes! she warbles loudly
   The thoughts that were my own;
The secret of my bosom
   To all the wood is known.

„Die Wellen blinken und fließen dahin."

THE waters glitter and glide away,—
　Love is lovely when spring is shining!
By the stream a shepherdess sits all day,
　The tenderest garlands twining.

Here are sweet blooms and the hum o' the bee,—
　Love is lovely when spring is shining!
The shepherdess sighs from her heart, 'Ah me!
　For whom are my garlands twining?'

By comes a trooper; with kindly grace
　He greets her as on he prances,
The maiden looks up with a wistful face,
　His gay plume flutters and dances.

She weeps, and into the river flings
　The garlands she sat a-twining;
Of love and kisses the nightingale sings—
　Love is lovely when spring is shining.

„Leise zieht durch mein Gemüth."

SWEETLY in my heart doth sing
　Fairy-like bell-tinkling:
Ring out, little song of spring,
　Music gaily sprinkling!

Fleetly hie yon cottage nigh,
　Where, with flowerets meeting,
If a Rose thou floatest by,
　Breathe my tender greeting.

„Wo wird einst des Wandermüden."[1]

WHERE then shall I rest for ever,
    Worn and weary of my day?
Under lindens by Rhine river?
    Under palm-trees far away?

Shall I, in the desert dying,
    Buried be by stranger hands?
Or, on some lone sea-coast lying,
    Slumber in the shifting sands?

Ah well! God's own heaven will brighten
    There as here above my bed;
And at night the stars will lighten—
    Glorious death-lamps o'er my head.

[1] A posthumous poem.

PART II.

Miscellaneous Pieces

BY

VARIOUS GERMAN POETS.

MISCELLANEOUS PIECES.

SPRING SONG.

Who shakes against my window here
  The green twigs gaily glancing?
The merry breeze of morn is near,
  And with the leaves is dancing.

Up! up! thou child of earth, to thee
  Thy sprightly mate appealeth,
As full of Spring it roveth free,
  And past thy threshold stealeth.

And hear'st thou not the beetles' hum?
  Hear'st not the tinkling ticking,
When, drunk with light and sweets, they come,
  Against thy window clicking?

Shall frolic sunbeams steal in vain
  Through leaves and branches to thee?
With dazzling waving and twinkling, fain
  Would they from slumber woo thee.

The nightingale she sung so long,
  Her fainting notes I pitied;
And since thou didst not hear her song,
  Away the sweet bird flitted.

Here at thy window, here I call,
  With idle branches beating,
Up! up! for Spring is over all,
  And ah! its glance is fleeting.

WILHELM MÜLLER.

A CHANGE.

Heart, my heart, what doth undo thee?
   Why this changed and troubled lot?
Strange new life is pulsing through thee;
   Life so strange, I know thee not.
All thy old desires are banish'd,
All thy vexing thoughts have vanish'd,
Zeal and rest alike I miss—
Ah, how cam'st thou, heart, to this?

Is it youth, with beauty beaming,
   That dear form hath captured thee?
Must that glance with goodness gleaming
   Ever thy enslaver be?
Should I think no more to see her,
Gather heart, and stoutly flee her—
Ah! the very path I track
In a moment leads me back.

By this magic thread, that surely
   Will not break, I'm holden still;
And that roguish one securely
   Keeps me thus against my will.
Ne'er her magic circle quitting,
I must live to do her bidding;
Ah, how great a change to me!—
Cruel love! O set me free!

GOETHE.

NEW LIFE.

Ha! what feelings wake and flower,
   In my happy bosom seated!
Ha! before what sun of power
   Hath my life's dark night retreated!
Golden sweet the greetings be
From this rosy dawn to me.

Yonder to my lifted eyes
   Paradise doth bloom and glisten;
To glad music from the skies
   Breathless here I stand and listen;
Eden's amaranthine air
Breathes around me everywhere.

Art so near me, god of wine,
   At life's feast my kind protector,
Turning this poor cup of mine
   To ambrosia and to nectar?—
Giver of these gifts divine—
Art so near me, god of wine?

Love! O wonder-working love!
   Thou to me new life hast given,
Raising this poor heart above
   To the happiness of heaven;
O unchanged with thee to rest,
Ever young and ever blest!

BÜRGER.

NO ANSWER.

When earth in the sweet Spring-time awakes,
    What feeling of bliss hath she?
When from dark woods a brooklet breaks,
    What can its musings be?

And what thinks the rose, the rose overnight
    That oped its breast to the dew?
And when a maiden wakes to love's light,
    What thrilleth her bosom through?

I ask'd the rose, and then the brook,
    And I ask'd the shining earth;
And they smiled on me with a joyous look,
    But dumb were they all in their mirth.

Then I ask'd my love, whose little head
    Hath so much wisdom conn'd,
Yet never a word my darling said,
    But kiss'd me, silent and fond.

A little tear stole down her cheek,
    Happy she look'd on me—
Now I think in my heart, Shall I further seek,
    Or shall this an answer be?

                    ROBERT REINICK.

THE SECRET WILL OUT.

Speed on! speed on! my winsome grey,
    How slow thy gallop seemeth!
Haste, haste with me and my secret away
    To where the wildwood gleameth.

O red and rosy the cloudlets flee
    Yon glimmering mountains over!
O sweetly lilts from every tree
    Each blithesome little rover!

And O like the lark from earth to spring,
    A gladsome, jubilant spirit!
'Mong the rosy clouds my joy to sing
    Till all the heavens should hear it.

Or a mighty wingèd storm to be,
    To rouse the dark blue ocean,
And confide to the waves of the surging sea
    This sweet and glowing emotion!

No ear shall hear it; I cannot hie
    Like a lark on the wing to quiver,
Nor over the waves like the tempest fly—
    And yet I must whisper it ever.

Listen, ye beeches! thou moon, hear this,
    In the weltering water captured—
She is mine! she is mine! her burning kiss
    Glows on my lips enraptured.

EMANUEL GEIBEL.

SECRECY.

Ah, if love thy bosom presses,
    Never let that love be known;
Deep within thy heart's recesses,
    Keep it to thyself alone.

See! yon mountain ne'er revealeth
   Where the golden treasures lie,
But its secret mine concealeth
   Safely from the intruder's eye.

And the pearls like sweet thoughts cluster,
   Sleeping in a dusky shell,
No eye marks their shrouded lustre
   In the dark house where they dwell.

And unseen thy heart abideth
   In its passion and its rest;
All unmark'd the giant hideth
   With the secrets of thy breast.

Thus let love, unseen and lonely,
   Nestle in thy bosom's shrine;
Tell the balmy secret only
   To the loved one that is thine.

To the blind yon heavens discover
   Nothing of their starry sheen;
And by no one save a lover
   Can love's loveliness be seen.

CARL DRÄXLER-MANFRED.

PARTING.

MAUN I then, maun I then to the toun awa',
   And we twae parted be?
When I come, when I come, when I come again,
   Nae mair I'll gae frae thee.

Though wi' thee I canna ever bide,
    Thou art yet my heart to me ;
When I come, when I come, when I come again,
    I will gae nae mair frae thee.

Sair thou greets, sair thou greets that I maun awa',
    Just as if our loves were by :
In yon toun, in yon toun mony lassies be,
    But, my hinnie, true am I.
Dinna think when I anither see
    That my love will a' blaw by :
In yon toun, in yon toun mony lassies be,
    But, my hinnie, true am I.

At the hairst, at the hairst, when they strip the trees,
    Back again I'll come to thee ;
Aye the same, aye the same, thy sweetheart still ;
    Then shall our wedding be.
Hairst weel owre, then is my service by,
    I'm bound to nane but thee ;
Aye the same, aye the same, thy sweetheart still—
    O wedded we shall be !

VOLKSLIED.

PRESENCE IN ABSENCE.

I THINK of thee when far o'er ocean shimmers
      Day's golden gleam ;
I think of thee when in the fountain glimmers
      The pale moonbeam.

I see thee when the frolic dust-cloud quivers
    In dreamy light ;
When on the narrow bridge the wanderer shivers
    In the deep night.

I hear thee when the rushing billows glisten
    And burst in foam ;
Oft in yon silent grove for thee I listen
    When all is dumb.

I'm with thee, love! Though far away thou'rt dreaming,
    Yet art thou near!
The sun goes down, soon will the stars be gleaming—
    O wert thou here!

GOETHE.

THE SOLDIER'S LOVE.

As still at midnight, dark and deep,
My lonely watch and ward I keep,
I think of her, my little pet,
And wonder if she loves me yet.

She kiss'd me tenderly that day
When to the wars I would away ;
With ribbons gay my hat she dress'd,
And, weeping, drew me to her breast.

She loves me still—yes, true is she ;
No dark foreboding troubles me ;
My heart beats warm i' the cold night air
When thinking of my faithful fair.

Perchance this is the very hour
Thy lamp is lit within thy bower,
And thou dost kneel to God and pray
For me, thy lover, far away.

And if war's perils wake thy fears,
And thou be sad, and full of tears,
Fear not, for God shall keep me through,
He loves a soldier good and true.

But, hark, a bell! relief is near,
My watch will soon be over here;
Now peaceful may thy slumbers be,
And in thy dreamings think of me.

WILHELM HAUFF.

AN EVIL CONSCIENCE.

'Warm are thy kisses, bright thine eye,
  I lean upon thy breast;
But ever upon thy brow doth lie
  A dark cloud of unrest.

'I love thee as loveth the river its vale,
  As ocean its golden sand,
As fairies the moonlight in the dale,
  As the hungry flame its brand.

'I love thee as loveth the world sweet day,
  And deeper and truer still—
Then chide me not, but say, O say
  What griefs thy bosom thrill.'

'Proud is thy beauty, bright thine eye,
   And warm is thy spirit in thee;
O fair! O noble! thine every sigh
   Breathes infinite love for me.

'And ah! what pains me wouldst thou know?
   What secret shades my brow?—
A blue-eyed little one long ago
   I loved as I love thee now.

'I loved her as loveth the river its vale,
   As ocean its golden sand,
As fairies the moonlight in the dale,
   As the hungry flame its brand.

'I loved her as loveth the world sweet day,
   And deeper and truer my sigh—
O shudder not, sweet! but hear me say,
   I loved, yet faithless was I.

'My brow is dark, my heart is sore,
   Restless I tremble, and say:
Thou lovest me as I loved before,—
   And that old love faded away.'

MORITZ GRAF STRACHWITZ.

THE THREE ROSES.

I sit me doun by a spring,
   Nae thirst hae I;
I seek a fause-hearted love,
   She comes na by.

And here am I a' my lane
   'Mang the greenerie:
Upo' my breist fa' doun
   Reid roses three.

I look a' round and aboon
   Wi' anxious een;
I hae my fause-hearted love
   Wi' anither seen.

She throws the roses to him
   On me that licht;
She thinks they 're a' alane—
   I 'm a waefu' wicht!

To see anither wi' her,
   This pains me sair;
Ah, thee, my fause-hearted love,
   I 'll see nae mair!

I 'll gae, and paper and pen
   And ink I 'll buy,
And write to my fause-hearted love
   Fareweel for aye.

And could ye sae soon gae awa'
   And lichtly me?—
I gae, my fause-hearted love,
   Far, far frae thee.

And noo I lay me adoun
   'Mang the hay and straw,
And saftly there on my breist
   Three roses fa'!

And thae three roses, I wat,
  Are bluid bluid reid:
I kenna whether my love
  Be livin' or deid.

VOLKSLIED.

DESOLATION.

LITTLE flower, in thy narrow dell,
Light from heaven on thy beauty fell:
Woful heart in thy aching breast,
Love with thee once found a rest.

And the floweret droops and pines
For the sun no longer shines;
And the heart doth break at last,
For the short-lived joy is past.

ALBERT TRAEGER.

THE OLD OAK-TREE.

THERE's a grand old oak in the low countrie
  Shines bright in its summer green;
Ah, many a time by that old oak-tree
  Have I with my true love been.

There's a dear wee bird would whistle there
  Till sweetly the welkin rang,
And my darling and I oft linger'd near
  To hear what the wee bird sang.

To the topmost bough the wee bird took
    To rest his little wing;
And he hush'd his note till he saw us look,
    Then he could not choose but sing.

The wee bird slept in his cosie nest,
    When the leaves had ceased to gleam—
O love! have I ever thy bosom press'd.
    Or is this but an idle dream?

I came again to my love, my bride—
    The tree was dead at last;
And a stranger walk'd by the dear one's side—
    O yes! I had dream'd the past.

The old oak stands in the low countrie,
    While, forsaken and forsaking,
Where the mountain snows lie drearilie,
    There my heart, my heart, is breaking.

VOLKSLIED.

UNREST.

WILD heart so oft deceivèd, tell me now
    What means this frenzied beating in my breast?
After such anguish past, say, wilt not thou
        Calm thee to rest?

Youth is gone by, its joys have sunk in night,
    With rosy blooms life's tree hath ceased to gleam;
Ah, what once raised thee to yon heaven of light
        Was but a dream!

The blossoms fell, for me was left the thorn,
    From whose sharp wound the blood flows evermore;
Now grief, and yearning, and an angry scorn
        Are all my store.

And yet were one to bring me Lethe's tide,
    And say, 'Drink thou, and all thy pain will go,
And soft forgetfulness the past will hide'—
        I'd answer, No!

For were it but an idle dream, yet I
    Know it was fair and sweet all else above;
Deep, deep I feel in every breath and sigh
        That still I love!

Then let me go! and, heart, still bleed amain!
    Yearning I seek a spot by night and day,
Where with my closing song this grief and pain
        May sigh away.

EMANUEL GEIBEL.

CALM AFTER STORM.

ALL the day long hath she raged and raved,
    As if in wrath and pain;
Now calm, and smoothing her ruffled breast,
    Slumbers the billowy main.

Gently goeth the evening wind
    Over the watery lea:
It is the breath of God that moves,
    Lulling the slumbering sea.

It kisses her curlèd tresses there,
  That late were streaming wild,
And the whisper'd blessing tenderly falls—
  'Sleep now, thou wayward child.'

MORITZ GRAF STRACHWITZ.

WINTER DREAMS.

My soul is gently shaken
  With a yearning sweet as May,
And in my heart awaken
  Bright dreams of a summer day.

I think of woods as they glisten
  At golden eve, and seem
In their glades to lie and listen
  To the distant horn, and dream.

I feel as I were sinking
  In the coolest grass e'er grew,
And from sweet cups were drinking
  Rare draughts of pearly dew.

Methinks I see heaven beaming
  With the light of dying day;
While the clouds on its breast are gleaming,
  And the little birds haste away.

And I seem to ask these, smiling,
  Whither away haste ye,
While I, the hours beguiling,
  Lie sunk in a flowery sea?

Oh, I feel in this dark weather
   Sweet thoughts of the past awake,
Old dreams and songs together
   Will over my bosom break.

Ah, why should earth and heaven
   Only bloom in our bosoms so,
And into our paths be driven
   The dreary winter snow?

EDUARD FERRAND.

THE NUN.

High on a hill I rested,
   And gazed into a vale;
I saw three knights in a shallop
   Adown a river sail.

The youngest of the rovers
   In that fair companie,
The wine from his own wine-cup
   He once did give to me.

What took he from his finger?—
   A ring of gold so bright—
'And keep it ever, fair one,
   For sake of thy true knight.'

'What shall I with the ring, Sir?
   Few summers have I told;
I'm but a poor young maiden,
   With neither goods nor gold.'

'Art thou a poor young maiden?
  Hast neither goods nor gold?
Think ever of the rich love
  Our faithful bosoms hold.'

'I do not know what love is,
  I think of ne'er a one—
So will I to the cloister
  And there become a nun.'

'And wilt thou to the cloister,
  A little nun to be?
So through the world I'll wander
  And come again to thee.'

When three months were nigh passèd
  He dream'd a dreary dream—
Shut up within the cloister
  His little love did seem.

The knight call'd to his henchman,
  'Go saddle our steeds in haste;
We'll take the way, as well we may
  By dale and mountain waste.'

And when he came to the cloister,
  He knock'd with meikle fear:
'Where is the youngest sister
  Was last to enter here?'

But no one comes to his bidding—
  An angry man is he—
'Oh, I will burn the cloister,
  God's house although it be!'

Thus loudly call'd, she cometh,
    All clad in white, and pale;
Gone are her sunny tresses:
    The maid has ta'en the veil.

Gently she bids them welcome
    Into this strange countrie—
'Who was it bade ye hither?
    Whose messengers are ye?'

Then woful, woful was the knight,
    Her words did vex him so:
He turn'd away, while down his cheeks
    The warm tears bitter flow.

What holds she in her hands there?—
    A golden cup to drain;
But hardly had he touch'd the cup
    Ere broke his heart in twain.

With her white hands the maiden
    Dug for the knight a grave;
And holy water from her eyes,
    Her dark brown eyes, she gave.

Her sweet voice in soft dirges
    Sang o'er the sleeper's head;
Her sweet voice was the little bell
    That toll'd above his bed.

VOLKSLIED.

THE LANDLADY'S DAUGHTER.

OVER the Rhine went students three,
And quickly came to an hostelrie.

'Landlady! hast thou good beer and wine?
Where is that little daughter of thine?'

'My beer and wine are clear and bright;
My daughter sleeps in her shroud so white.'

The inner chamber they drew near,
And saw the little one on her bier.

The first laid aside the veil to gaze
With sadden'd look on the dear one's face:

'Ah, wert thou living now, sweet May!
My heart I know would be thine this day.'

The second he cover'd her face again,
And weeping turn'd him away in pain:

'Ah, thou that liest on thy bier,
I have loved thee, sweet, for many a year.'

The third once more raised up the veil,
And kiss'd the lips so cold and pale:

'I love thee now as I loved before,
I love thee, love, for evermore.'

UHLAND.

LOVE'S LEGACY.

O Spring it is so fair and bright
  With sunshine, buds, and song;
Since swift away it wings its flight,
  Nor ever tarries long.

And ah! so sweet the rosy glow
    O'er love's first dreamings shed,
Since fleeter than the flowerets go
    These rosy dreams are fled.

Yet round that heart warm treasures twine
    Where young love bloom'd and gleam'd;
A happy luck I think is mine
    That I have loved and dream'd.

Beam after beam my heart hath ta'en
    From this too fleeting day;
But though the sun be on the wane,
    Yet, come whatever may,

And still I'll bear a steadfast mind,
    Be grief or joy in store—
The treasure in my heart enshrined
    Is mine for evermore.
EMANUEL GEIBEL.

DAME NIGHTINGALE.

NIGHTINGALE, thy vesper keeping,
While thou singest I am weeping;
Pretty lady Nightingale,
Thee a thousand times I hail!

Nightingale, I see thee hasten
To this fountain's rocky basin,
There to dip that bill of thine,
Deeming this the best of wine.

Nightingale, say which is better—
On the linden tops to twitter;
Or amid green boughs to rest
In thy dainty little nest?

Now, again, thy notes are ringing!
How delicious is thy singing!
Come to me, and tell me true
What, sweet lady, can I do?

Dost thou, then, in sorrow languish?
Come, and I will heal thine anguish;
Bid thy fancies all be gone—
Where does thy belovèd won?

Thou shalt find him, little lady, —
Leave thy bowers cool and shady,
Seek on hill and seek on plain—
Greet him o'er and o'er again.

VOLKSLIED.

THE LAUREL AND THE ROSE.

Let the laurel, if he choose,
   Crown each poet ever;
Nor a chain of gold refuse
   Critics sharp and clever.

Give me but the rose, love-fraught,
   There all sweetness slumbers;—
Love only was the Muse that taught
   Me to lisp in numbers.

ERNST SCHULZE.

THE WATER LILIES.

The lilies in the lonesome lake
   Cluster in gleaming masses;
They wave and play the livelong day
   With every breeze that passes;
But when the night puts day to flight,
And in yon heavens the moon is bright,
Like nymphs from out the waters,
Dance forth the lake's pale daughters.

Now rings the wind, now sings the reed,
   And to the music sweetly
The lily maidens twine themselves
   In wreaths, and foot it fetely.
Round in a ring they sweep and sail,
With robes and faces white and pale,
Until each wan cheek flushes
With tender rosy blushes.

Loud rings the wind, loud sings the reed,
   Forth woodland echoes sally,
And clouds are strewn across the moon,
   And shadows o'er the valley.
And to and fro the mad ones reel,
Through grass and dew they whirl and wheel;
And loud and louder calleth
The wavelet where it falleth.

But lo! an arm, with giant fist,
   From out the water springeth,
And crown'd with reeds a dripping head,
   To which a long beard clingeth.

And now a voice in thunder thrills
The slumbering echoes of the hills:—
'Back! back! pale lily-daughters,
And hide you 'neath the waters.'

Their frolics cease; the maidens shriek,
    And pale become as ever:
The father cries:—'Waft, morning sighs,
    Athwart each lake and river.'
Swift from the vale the mists are gone,
The skies are flushing with the dawn:
And in the lake the lilies toy,
And wave and flutter in their joy.

AUGUST SCHNETZLER.

THE ROSEBUD.

The rosebud dreams of the sunny sheen,
Of the rustle of leaves in forest green,
Of the musical fall of fairy springs,
And the dainty song the nightingale sings,
Of the breeze that laughs and dances for joy,
And the blooms that tenderly woo and toy.
The rosebud wakes, in beauty appears
And gently smiles through her shining tears;
And she looks and listens, for all is bright,
And there's music and rustling, and balmy delight;
Her dreams have come true—her beautiful dreams—
    And all in a tremulous wonder is she,
As softly she whispers—'Truly it seems
    As were not new all this beauty to me.'

FRIEDRICH VON SALLET.

THE DYING FLOWER.

'Hope that thou shalt live to see
   Spring and sunshine come again;
E'en as hopeth every tree
   Stript by autumn winds and rain.
In thy heart a secret power
   Sleepeth through the wintry gloom;
When the sky has ceased to lower
   It shall wake, and thou shalt bloom.'

'Ah, I am no forest king,
   Living down a thousand years,
Through whose winter dreams doth ring
   Sweet May-music, drowning fears—
No! a little flower am I,
   Waken'd by the kiss of May,
Ere the snows about me lie
   I must faint and fade away.'

'Though thou art a tender flower,
   Wherefore needst thou sigh or care,
Are not seeds the heavenly dower,
   Thou and all thy sisters share?
Let the winter winds and rimes
   Rudely lay thee in the tomb,
From the sod a thousand times
   Thou shalt rise, and bud, and bloom.'

'Yes, full many a flower, I ween,
   After me in light will rise;
Earth is green, for ever green,
   But each little green thing dies.

They will shine, as I have shone—
   I who nothing was before;
Now I live—when I am gone,
   I am gone for evermore.

'When the sunshine o'er their bloom
   Blazes as it blazes yet,
'Twill not mitigate my doom—
   In dark night for ever set.
Ah, thou Sun! e'en now thy gleam
   Seems to hail them ere they glow;
Wherefore with a frosty beam
   Dost thou mock me while I go?

'Thee I trusted—woe is me!
   When thou kiss'd me into day:
And I look'd with love to thee;
   But thou filch'd my life away.
From thy pity will I hide
   What poor life thou yet hast left:
Closing my weak leaves, I bide
   In myself till I am reft.

'Yet the ice about my heart
   Thou dost melt to tears that shine,—
Thou who ever living art,
   Take this fleeting life of mine!
Yes, thou sunnest all the woe
   From this fainting life and me;
And I thank thee while I go—
   All my beauty came from thee!

'Every zephyr floating by
   That I sweetly breathed upon,
Every twinkling butterfly
   Dancing round my starry crown;
Eyes that brighten'd at my sheen,
   Hearts that for my balm would sigh—
Thou didst give me all, I ween,
   And I thank thee ere I die.

'Though I was a lowly birth,
   Yet I deck'd this world of thine,
And thou bad'st me bloom on earth,
   As the stars in heaven shine.
One breath draw I while I yield,
   And a sigh it shall not be;
One look have I for the field,
   One for heaven and for thee.

'Ever-burning heart o' the world,
   Let me fade into thy light!
Heaven's blue covering be unfurl'd
   While my green one shrinks in night!
Hail, thou morn, with balmy breath!
   Hail, O Spring, thou golden reign!
Calmly now I sleep in death,
   Nevermore to wake again!'

FRIEDRICH RÜCKERT.

THE MAIDEN AND THE BUTTERFLY.

It was a happy maiden
    Walk'd in a woodland fair,
And as she gather'd posies,
Sweet violets and roses,
A butterfly alighted
    And kiss'd the maiden there.

'Forgive me,' said the flutterer,
    'If I've done aught amiss:
The day it is so sunny
That I would gather honey,
And thy lips, red and dainty,
    I did for roses kiss.'

Then said the little maiden,
    'For this time lightly go!
And I forgive thee fully:—
But mark! I tell thee truly,
That not for every flutterer
    These dainty roses blow.'

                      R. C. WEGENER.

THE DAYS OF THE ROSES.

Now is the blooming and golden time!—
O world so wide in thy beautiful prime!
O deep, wide heart! O day so fair!
How the lark's song rings through the joyous air!

Let life's sweet May in the bosom chime—
Now is the beautiful blooming time—
  Now are the days of the roses!

And free is the heart, and free is song,
And free is the youth who travels along,
And rosy kisses are not less free
Though bashful and coy the lips may be.
Where a kiss may be had, where a song doth chime,
Take them! for now is the golden time—
  Now are the days of the roses!

Ah, deep in the heart is everything grown—
There the seeds of joy and sorrow are sown:
And what though our bosoms be peaceful and gay,
Soon tempests will rage and peace fly away:
Yet prompt are we ever to sing this rhyme—
Now is the beautiful golden time!—
  Now are the days of the roses!

OTTO ROQUETTE.

THE DUET.

'TWAS an elder-tree, and a bird sat there,
  In a calm and beautiful night in May;
In the grass beneath was a maiden fair,
  In a calm and beautiful night in May.
While the wee bird listen'd the maiden sang,
When the maiden ceased then the bird's note rang,
        And far away
        Their roundelay
Waken'd the vale where the moonbeams stray.

What sang the bird upon the tree,
   In that calm and beautiful night in May?
And the little maiden, what sang she,
   In that calm and beautiful night in May?—
The wee bird warbled of Spring so bright,
And the maiden sang of love's delight;
      Ah, how their lay
      Round my heart did play!
'Twill live in my bosom for ever and aye!

ROBERT REINICK.

SONG.

How gladly at thy feet, love,
   I sing my sweetest lay,
While through the window golden beams
   At holy even stray.
Thy little head beats time to me,
   Still'd is thy listening heart:
I fold my hands and sing, love—
   'How wondrous fair thou art!'

How gladly at thy feet, love,
   I gaze up at thine eyes;
Soft pity seems to tremble there—
   But spare, love, spare thy sighs!
For well I know 'tis but thy play,
   And yet I cannot part,
But kneel before thee singing—
   'How wondrous fair thou art!

How gladly at thy feet, love,
   In dumb grief could I die;
But rather would I, leaping up,
   A thousand kisses try!
Yes, I could kiss thee, kiss thee, love,
   A whole long day to my heart,
And, sinking down, die singing—
   'How wondrous fair thou art!'

MORITZ GRAF STRACHWITZ.

WANDERING.

THE happy trees are blooming, sweet May is come again,
Now bide at home who like it, with sorrow and pain!
But as the clouds wander in the sunny summer day,
So through the wide world I'll ramble far away.

Dear father! dear mother! God keep you evermore!
Who knows what luck for me elsewhere may be in store?
There's many a road by which I never hied,
And many a wine too I never yet have tried.

Up! up, then, and off! while the golden cloudlets sail,
I'll over the mountains and through the dewy dale;
The cool fountains tinkle, the trees they swing and toy,
Like a lark my heart is soaring and singing in its joy.

At evening, all athirst, I reach a hostel sign—
'Ho, landlord, master landlord; a cup of white wine!
And you, merry fiddler, strike up a cheery lay,
And I will a sing a song about my own dear may.'

And when I find no lodging, I lie in the sight
Of the dark blue heavens, where the stars watch all night;
The breeze with the trees my lullaby doth make,
And the rosy blush of morning kisses me awake.

O wandering! O wandering! how truly am I blest!
Now breathes the breath of heaven fresh in my breast!
O the music! O the rapture about me that are hurl'd—
How beautiful and bounteous is the wide, wide world!

EMANUEL GEIBEL.

THE APPRENTICE SETTING OUT.

WHAT ringing and singing is that in the street?
Ye maidens, open your windows to greet
The youth of whom Fortune bereaves us,
And give him a smile ere he leaves us.

Loud shout his comrades, and cheer him along,
Troops of young fellows, a generous throng;
He recks not the din that still groweth,
But pale in the midst there he goeth.

Loud clink the tankards and sparkles the wine—
'Drink once and drink often, dear brother mine!'
'While the parting-cup kindly is flowing
Die the thoughts in my soul that are glowing!'

From the corner house at the end of the street,
A maiden looks out the sad youth to greet;
Her tears she hides in her posies—
Her violets rare and her roses.

And there at this house as he passes by,
The youth looks up with a sorrowful eye;
And she looks down, trembling blossom,
And lays her hand on her bosom.

'Ah, brother, and hast thou no posy rare,
While so many blooms are nodding up there?—
Ho, pretty one! pluck him a flower,
Let it fall at his feet from thy bower.'

'Ah, brothers! and what is a flower to me?
I have no sweetheart, comrades, as ye!
The flower in the sunshine will wither,
And the winds blow it hither and thither.'

And further, still further, with ringing and song,
And the maiden listens, and listens long;
'Woe is me! in his going have perish'd
The hopes that in secret I cherish'd.

'Here stood I with this love of mine,
With violets rare and with eglantine,
And all would I give him with gladness,
Now afar he wanders in sadness.'

UHLAND.

HIDDEN PAIN.

My luve's been awa' this mony a day—
And oh! I canna tell—but my heart's sae wae!
It's maybe that he's deid, and sleepin' sound, sound,
That maks life to me sic a drearie round.

When to the kirk we 'd gae, my luve and I,
There fause, spitefu' tongues stood clypin' by;
And ane said this, and anither said that—
And oh! but aften and sair I grat!

The nettle and the thorn they never stung
Sae shairp and sae sair as a fause, spitefu' tongue;
And there 's nae fire on earth will e'er burn or blaw
Sae warm as the luve that 's hidden frae a'.

Ah, luve, my luve, come back again, and be
At my side when kirkwards they carry me—
At my side when they lay me the green grass amang,
For weel hae I lo'ed thee my hale life lang.

Ah, what gart my faither and mither dae this?—
They forced me to wed against my wis—
To wed when my heart wasna mine to gie,
Sae weary and sae dreary now is life to me.

VOLKSLIED.

THE LINDEN-TREE.

Hard by yon bubbling fountain
   There stands a linden-tree,
And often 'neath its shadow
   Sweet dreams have come to me.

Ah, many a tender love-word
   That dear old linden bore,
And still in joy or sorrow
   It woos me as of yore.

This night, when all is silent,
   I pass that linden by,
Where often in my childhood
   I have closed the weary eye.

Hark! how its boughs are calling,
   As they tremble to my breast,
'Come here to me, old comrade,
   Come here, and find thy rest!'

The biting winds they buffet
   And strike me on the face;
They bare my head—I heed not,
   But ever onward pace.

Far, far now have I wander'd
   From yonder linden-tree;
But still I hear it calling—
   'Come back and rest with me!'

WILHELM MÜLLER.

THE ELDER-TREE.

WHERE the frolic wind goes fresh and free,
High on yon hill, stands an elder-tree,
   Over the green earth bending.

The breeze is cool, and the night is fair,—
Two tearful lovers are lingering there,
   For the hour has come to part them.

And, weeping, they tear themselves away—
O weary and sad at heart are they!
   And they met no more for ever.

And he went over the dark, broad sea,
And a fearful tale of death heard she;
   And far o'er the hill she wander'd.

Their very names are lost, O woe !
Only the moon their graves doth know,
   There the summer winds are straying.

And still on the hill stands the elder-tree,
All bright with blossoms and fair to see,
   Over the green earth bending.

OTTO ROQUETTE.

EVENING SONG.

On a swelling hill I rested,—
   The sun was sinking low;
And I saw the woodland vested
   In even's golden glow.

As heaven to earth drew nearer,
   Sweet peace with the dew-drop fell;
And forth came Sleep, the cheerer,
   At the sound of the evening bell.

And I said :—O heart, tired Nature
   Now calms its throbbing breast;
Do thou with every creature
   Be still, and take thy rest.

The flowers in yonder meadows
   Have closed their eyes to dream,
And the wavelets 'neath the shadows
   Low ripple adown the stream.

The caterpillar creepeth
  'Neath its tiny leaf to lie;
Among the rushes sleepeth
  The dew-drench'd dragon-fly.

The golden beetle lieth
  In a rose-leaf, cradled light;
With his flock the shepherd hieth
  To rest in the gathering night.

Low in the dewy clover
  The lark sits hush'd in its nest;
And the hart, all day a rover,
  With the hind lies down to rest.

Now every one repaireth
  To where his fireside beams;
And he who in far lands fareth
  Yet homeward goes in dreams.

But this thought in my heart is swelling—
  While all things restful be,
Heaven's sweet and peaceful dwelling
  Is far away from me.

FRIEDRICH RÜCKERT.

AUTUMN.

The leaves are falling yonder,
  As, at the close of day,
In silent dreams I wander
  Along the rocky way.

Swift flee the bright clouds, flaring
   Wild in the golden light,
For storms afar preparing—
   Their glory fades in night.

The wandering birds are driven
   In flickering swarms to gain
Some brighter, balmier heaven,
   And the year is on the wane.

Unseen the flowers are dying
   Where the darkling waters stray,
And the last dew-drops are sighing
   From their fainting bloom away.

Old times we so yearn after
   Glide with the clouds along—
Where are the tears and laughter
   And the kindly word and song?

Winds rave, the leaves down-beating;—
   I care not, let them play!
The days like dreams are fleeting,
   And the joys have pass'd away.

                HERMANN LINGG.

ONWARD.

SIGH not o'er the days departed,
   Nor old times wish back again;
In the present live, brave-hearted—
   Tears for vanish'd joys are vain.

Steer thy bark serene, securely,
  All the world before thee lies;
Striving, suffering, hoping, surely
  Thou shalt gain the distant prize.

Woe to him who, weak, despairing,
  Sighs for moments past recall—
In his own strength never daring,
  But the present blames for all—

Who with anxious fear and sorrow,
  Ever looketh back in pain!—
Golden fair beyond the morrow
  Gleams the bright land thou must gain.

Onward! onward! by such straining
  Was the Golden Fleece secured;
So shalt thou, the haven attaining,
  Grasp the prize thy youth assured.

Sigh not o'er the days departed,
  Nor old times wish back again;
In the present live, brave-hearted—
  Tears for vanish'd joys are vain.

HEINRICH ZEISE.

LONGINGS.

Sweet days, dear hours, now lost to me for ever!
  Ah happy youth and blooming time!
Come, blessed Fancy! through my bosom quiver,
  And give me back in dreams my golden prime.

Float nigh, thou morning, with thy gleam and glory,
    That woo'd me forth upon my way :
Ah, then life seem'd a beautiful, bright story—
    No care, no grief to cloud the broadening day.

Dear innocence of childhood, float around me,
    Lost paradise of sinless hours !
Sweet hope ! how strong the ties to earth that bound me—
    That sunny earth, that wilderness of flowers !

How did I fold ye warm in my embraces,
    Friends of my youth, true heart to heart !
Where are ye gone, dear old familiar faces,
    That once in every frolic bore a part ?

Ah, many now the lonesome grave encloses,
    Each slumbers in his mother's arm ;
Ye pale wan cheeks, bloom bright again with roses !
    Once more, ye cold hearts, quicken and grow warm.

In vain ! in vain ! my yearning cannot waken
    The dead ones where they lowly lie :
Swift fade the flowers of life by rude winds shaken ;
    And we—we wither slowly when they die.

O sweet fair land, where flowers for ever blossom !
    Where time and death are all unknown !
O sweet fair land, far in thy happy bosom
    There would my yearning heart fain seek its own.

What though before mine eyes dark shades assemble,
    This night of time will soon be o'er ;
Thou restful land, how do I yearn and tremble
    To reach thy Sabbath on the golden shore !

A. MAHLMANN.

THE LITTLE SISTER.

There was a Margrave by the Rhine—
He had three daughters fair and fine.

The first was wedded in Netherland;
The next she mated near at hand.

The third with father and mother stayed
Till they in death were lowly laid.

Then forth she wanders far away,
And wist not where her sister lay.

She stands a merchant's house before,
And taps there gently at the door.

'Who stands out there? who knocks so light,
And wakes me from my sleep to-night?'

'A poor little maiden here you see,
That gladly would your handmaid be.'

'Too gay, methinks, thou dost appear,
Thou goest with young lords, I fear.'

'Ah no! ah no! that cannot be,
My good name is too dear to me.'

For half a year she hires the maid;
For seven years the maiden stay'd;

And when the seventh year had fled
The maiden she lay sick abed.

'Maiden, since ill thou mayest be,
Who are thy parents tell to me.'

'My father was Margrave by the Rhine,
My mother came of a kingly line.'

'Ah no! ah no! that cannot be,
Else wert thou youngest sister to me.'

'Since then my words untrue appear,
Step you before my little chest here;

'There on the lid the same words be,
As you with your own eyes may see.'

And as she reads the graven scroll,
Fast down her cheeks the tears do roll.

'Ah, hadst thou told me before this morn,
Velvet and silk shouldst thou have worn.'

'Velvet and silk are not for me,
Soon in the cold dark grave to be.'

'Ah, bring me wine! ah, bring me bread!
Or my youngest sister will be dead.'

'Sister, nor wine nor bread I heed,
A little coffin is all I need.'

And when the maiden was laid to rest,
There grew three lilies over her breast;

And under the middle one was writ,
'The little maid to her God is knit.'

VOLKSLIED.

THE TRIAL OF LOVE.

Deep in a dale a tree did grow,
'Twas braid aboon and sma' below:
Aneath its shade twa lovers sat,
And in their love their wae forgat.

'The hour has come that parts us twa;
For seven years I maun awa';'
'And maun thou bide sae lang frae me?
I'll wed nane other love but thee.'

When come and gane was the hin'most year,
She thinks her love maun soon be near:
Into her garden then she gaes,
And bides wi' care to see his face.

Underneath the trystin'-tree
She looks if there her love micht be;
Syne wanders on into a wood,
When by there comes a knicht sae proud.

'My bonnie lassie, God thee sain!
What dost thou here in the wood alane?
Do faither and mither flyte and ban?
Or tell me, is't thine ain guidman?'

'My faither and mither flyte me not,
And ne'er a guidman hae I got;
'Tis seven years and lang weeks three
Since my dear love he gaed frae me.'

'Yestreen when I rade thro' a toun,
Thy love had on his weddin'-goun;

Since that thy love has been untrue,
What ill wish dost thou wish him noo?'

'I wish him a' gude things that be,
As mony as leaves are on the tree;
I wish him years and years o' joy,
As mony as stars are in the sky.

'I wish him honours in great plentie,
As is the sand alang the sea;
I wish him as meikle luck and a'
As draps o' rain frae heaven fa'.'

What took he aff his finger there?
A ring o' gold sae reid and fair;
Into her bosom this he threw,
Then wat were her cheeks wi' pearly dew.

What frae his pocket did he draw?
A napkin white as the drifted snaw,—
'Noo wipe thy cheek and dry thine e'e,
Nane other love will I hae but thee!

'I did but try thee, love, to see
An thou wouldst ban or lichtly me:
And hadst thou let ae wild word fa',
I had turn'd about and ridden awa'.'

VOLKSLIED.

THE DARK BROWN NIXIE.

A HUNTSMAN blew his hunting horn:
But he blew for nought—he was all forlorn.

'And if I must blow my horn for nought,
I had rather no huntsman be, I wot.'

Over a bush his net he flung,
From 'neath it a dark brown maiden sprung.

'Ah, dark brown maiden, flee not from me!
I have a hound will follow thee.'

'Thy hounds will do me no harm, I wot;
My tricks and doubles they know them not.'

'Thy tricks and doubles full well know they,
And they know that thou must die to-day.'

'And if I die, then, when I am dead,
Bury me under the roses red;

'Under the roses hidden away
I will not bide for ever and aye:

When I have long enough rested, then
Out of the grave will I rise again.'

There grew three lilies over this may,
By came a proud trooper would pluck them away.

Ah, leave the lilies where they have sprung,
They grow for a huntsman lusty and young.

VOLKSLIED.

THE INEXORABLE CAPTAIN.

O STRASSBURG, O Strassburg,
  Thou city proud and brave!
Full many a weary soldier
  In thee has found a grave.

Full many a soldier
  Of stout and hardy mind
His father and dear mother
  Has cruelly left behind.

So left them, so left them—
  It cannot but be so;
To Strassburg, yes, to Strassburg,
  The soldiers they must go!

The father and the mother
  They seek the Captain then:
'Ah, Captain, kind Sir Captain,
  Give me my son again!'

'Your son I cannot give you—
  No, not for gold will I;
Your son he must march with me
  When to the war I hie.

'To war then, afar then,
  E'en to the devil must he!
Ay, though his dark brown maiden
  Weep o'er him bitterly.'

With sighing and crying
  The maiden sobb'd full sore—
'Adieu, my heart's belovèd!
  Adieu for evermore!'

VOLKSLIED.

THE POET KING.

I know not what it means—before
I get beyond my cottage door
The lark to greet me upward springs,
And through the blue a triumph rings.

The grass and flowerets wait me there
With pearls and jewels in their hair;
And bush and corn and poplar-tree
Do ceremonious bow to me.

My messenger, the brooklet, darts;
And, as the wind the foliage parts,
Shy peeps the mead, and now will hide,
As if she were my own dear bride.

When, weary, I would roam no more,
The nightingale before the door
Doth serenade me; glow-worms light
The darkling forest in the night.

And truly now 'tis ever so,
No poet goes incognito;
Gay Spring doth quickly note who reigns
As king and lord in her domains.

JOSEPH FREIHERR VON EICHENDORFF.

THE CAPTIVE KNIGHT.

Two castles, old and towering,
  Glance in the sunny sheen,
They stand on cliffs opposing,
  And Rhine flows swift between.

And here a knight lies captive,
    And sick at heart is he,
For yonder wons his true love—
    His love he may not see.

He hears the river raving
    With restless onward flow,
And day by day for ever
    The waves they come and go.

He shakes the iron grating,—
    But firm the grating stands;
Vainly the door he forces
    With strong yet helpless hands.

His dear guitar he taketh
    Down from the wall again;
His joy when times were happier,
    His comfort now in pain.

Sad on his couch he sits there,
    And wakes and sighs; and light
His dear guitar he touches
    And sings alone i' the night.

        JOSEPH CHRISTIAN VON ZEDLITZ.

THE TWO COFFINS.

'NEATH the dome of an old Cathedral
    Lie two coffins side by side:
There a gentle poet sleepeth,
    And King Ottmar in his pride.

The king once high and mighty,
　On his father's throne sat he;
A sword they put in his right hand,
　And crown him for dignitie.

Yet side by side with the monarch
　Sleeps the gentle poet here,
His clay-cold hands still clasping
　The harp he held so dear.

Tower with tower is warring,
　Battle rings through the land,
But the rusting sword moves never,
　Lock'd in the pale king's hand.

Blooms and gentle breezes
　Breathe soft the vale along,
And the poet's harp resoundeth
　Its never-dying song.

　　　　　　　　JUSTINUS KERNER.

THE POET'S CONSOLATION.

No fond tear may trickle
　Where I lowly rest,
But the flowers will weep their
　Dews upon my breast.

No one there may linger
　Ere he passes by,
But soft beams will come there
　From the moonlit sky.

What though of my country
    I forgotten be!
Yet its groves and meadows
    They will think of me.

Flower, and grove, and meadow,
    Moon, and starry sheen,
They will keep their poet's
    Memory ever green.

JUSTINUS KERNER.

THE CASTLE BY THE SEA.

HAST thou seen the castle olden,
    High towering by the sea?
Crimson-bright and golden
    The clouds above it be.

Down stooping, it appeareth
    In the glassy wave below;
Its lofty towers it reareth
    Where the clouds of even glow.

Well have I seen it towering,
    That castle by the sea;
And the moon above it lowering,
    And the mists about it flee.

The winds and the waves rebounding,
    Say, rang they fresh and clear?
Heard'st thou from bright halls sounding
    Music and festal cheer?

The winds and waves were sleeping,
   But from that castle high
The sound of wailing and weeping
   Brought tears into mine eye.

Saw'st thou in grandeur gleaming
   The king and his lady queen?
And the purple mantles streaming?
   And the crowns with their golden sheen?

With rapturous love and tender,
   Led they a maiden there—
Bright as the sun in its splendour—
   Beaming with golden hair?

The king and queen, grief-laden,
   I saw, and their crowns were gone;
Sad weeds they wore,—no maiden
   Beside them in beauty shone.

UHLAND.

THE ANCESTRAL VAULT.

'Tis over the moorland dreary
   In the choir of the grey chapelle,
Paced a warrior old and weary
   Where the darksome shadows fell.

The coffins of his fathers
   Range all along the hall,
And a wondrous sound upgathers
   From where his footsteps fall.

'O glad I hear your greeting,
   Ye noble dead! and hie
To close your ranks—proud meeting!
   And worthy too am I.'

An empty coffin makes he
   To be his cold dark bed,
And for his pillow takes he
   The shield beneath his head.

His hand he dumbly places
   On his sword, and slumbers fain;
The ghostly greeting ceases,
   And peace and silence reign.

UHLAND.

THE BLIND KING.

WHY on that high and rocky shore
   Do these stout Norsemen stand?
What does the old king, blind and hoar,
   Amid that warrior band?
He leans, with anguish shaken,
   On 's staff, and loud cries he,
And his wild words awaken
   Yon island in the sea.

'Yield me, thou robber, from thy thrall
   My daughter good and true;
Her harp and song so sweet were all
   The joys of eld I knew.

From meadow-dance, rank riever!
  Thou snatch'd her o'er the sea;—
Dark shame awaits thee ever,
  And my heart dies in me.'

Out from his cave the robber flings,
  He scoffs, and scorns to yield;
Aloft his giant sword he swings
  And clashes on his shield.
'Stout guards thou hast a many—
  Why did they let me stir?
Strong swords—but never any
  Come here to fight for her!'

Tongue-tied they hear the taunt and boast,
  To brave him steppeth none;
The blind king turneth to his host—
  'Am I then all alone?'
But warm the young son graspeth
  His father's hand in his—
'O let me fight!' he gaspeth;
  'Strong is my arm for this!'

'My son, the fiend is stark and rough,
  Against him none may stand;
And yet—thou hast the noble stuff—
  I feel it in thy hand!
Take thou my sword, young Rover!
  That sword the minstrels sing,
And shouldst thou fall, then over
  Into the flood I spring!'

Swiftly the bark roars through the wave,
    Hark, how the waters foam!
The blind king stands and listens grave,
    And all around are dumb,
Till in yon isle the rattle
    Of sword and shield they hear,
And the wild din of battle,
    And echos loud and drear.

With anxious joy then cries the king,
    ' Now tell me what ye see!
My sword!—I know the good true ring:
    It strook with such a glee!'
' The robber's deeds are over,
    Sunk to his bloody grave;—
All hail to thee, young Rover!
    Thou bravest of the brave.'

Again the warriors silent stand,
    The blind king listens dumb—
' What hear I foaming to the strand?
    Who doth so swiftly come?'
' Here comes across the water
    Thy son with sword and shield,
Bringing thee back thy daughter,
    The sunny-hair'd Gunild.'

' Welcome!' from where the cliff uprears
    He cries across the wave;
' Now am I happy in my years,
    And honour'd in my grave.

My son! the good sword bring me,
  By this right hand to lie,
My dirge, sweet daughter! sing me;
  The blind old king will die!'

UHLAND.

THE NIBELUNGER'S TREASURE.

By Rhine, so goes the story,
  A king dwelt long ago;
And he was old and hoary,
  And hated wars and woe.

So long his nobles fought o'er
  A treasure in the land,
Ere the wild strife was got o'er
  Nigh kill'd were all the band.

He call'd them, as in duty,—
  'What matters gold, ye gulls,
If ye this golden booty
  Must pay for with your skulls?

'Go sink it in the river,
  And so end strife and care;
For ever and for ever
  Let it lie buried there.'

The cause of all the squabble
  Soon at the bottom lay,
In time the glittering bauble
  Was melted quite away.

It gave a sheen and lustre
    To Rhine as on he roll'd;
It swell'd the vine-tree's cluster,
    And made it gleam like gold.

And now may each one borrow
    A lesson from the king,
And ne'er let care or sorrow
    His manly bosom wring;

But bury all his troubles
    And quarrels in old Rhine,
And drink with joy the bubbles
    That sparkle in its wine.

VOLKSLIED.

THE POPE AND THE SULTAN.

The Pope a lordly state doth hold,
He never feels the want of gold,
Of wine the very best drinks he,—
O would that I the Pope might be!

Yet no! poor wight, he lacks one bliss—
A pretty lass he may not kiss;
Alone in his cold bed sleeps he—
So I the Pope don't wish to be.

The Sultan leads a jovial life,
With many a lovely lass to wife,
In a great palace by the sea—
So I the Sultan fain would be.

Yet no! poor man, he must be true
To what the Koran bids him do,
And never a drop of wine may pree—
So I the Sultan would not be.

Now each apart I somewhat scorn,
I'd rather live as I've been born—
But oh! 'twould be a joy to me
Could I half Pope, half Sultan be!

Come, give me, lass, your sweetest kiss,
And I'll be Sultan in my bliss!
And, comrades, let the wine flow free,
And I the lordly Pope will be!

VOLKSLIED.

CRAMBAMBULI.

CRAMBAMBULI, 'tis thus we christen
   The drink that sets our hearts aglow;
Whene'er we bid the nectar glisten
   Away our cares and troubles go.
And thus at morn and night, you see,
I drink my glass Crambambuli.

When at mine inn I have dismounted,
   Like some bold knight of old romaunt,
Your beef and bread for nought are counted—
   A corkscrew is my only want.
And while the horn sounds 'tan-tran-ti'
I quaff my glass Crambambuli.

When headache all my temper ruffles,
    And in my food I find no zest;
When I am bother'd with the snuffles,
    Or plagued with wheezing in the chest,
Your only medicine for me
Is just a glass Crambambuli.

Had I been born to power unbounded—
    An Emperor—then in a trice
An order fair I would have founded,
    With this for motto and device—
' Toujours fidèle et sans souci
C'est l'ordre du Crambambuli.'

When I at play am sorely bitten,
    And my poor purse is vilely bled:
When ne'er a word my lass hath written—
    But funeral letters come instead;—
My dumps and I at once agree
To bumpers of Crambambuli.

Ah, could the folk at home by thinking
    Guess at the need their sons must know:
How hard we strive to keep from sinking—
    Their tears for us would quickly flow;
But we meanwhile for comfort flee
And find it in Crambambuli.

An empty purse shall ne'er confound us,
    We'll take on tick from wealthy knaves,
Thinking 'tis vanity all round us,
    From students down to beggar slaves:

This is the prime philosophy
We suck from our Crambambuli.

When I for student-rights do battle,
   Or draw the sword for Fatherland,
Before the sabres round me rattle,
   I take my comrade by the hand :—
'Ere we begin, *mon cher ami,*
Let's have one glass Crambambuli.'

Ye prigs, who sneer at jovial glasses,
   Who love no love, who drink no wine ;
No hope have ye to be but asses,
   Although for saints ye think to shine ;
Swill, like the long-ear'd things ye be,
Swill water for Crambambuli.

When age comes on, and joys wax colder,
   I still will love a brimming cup,
And when Death taps me on the shoulder
   To tell me that my time is up,
I'll drink with him, *pour compagnie,*
One last fond glass Crambambuli.

STUDENTS' SONG.

THE MAN IN THE CELLAR.

In a cool cellar on a cask
   I sit enthroned and beaming,
To drink good wine my only task,
   And glory in its gleaming.

The drawer fills a brimming cup,
   Obedient to my winking;
I hold the sparkling beaker up—
   I'm drinking, drinking, drinking!

The demon Thirst disturbs my soul,
   And so, to scare the fellow,
I fill again the brimming bowl
   With Rhine-wine rich and mellow;
The whole round world now seems to me
   Through rosy colours blinking,—
I would do harm to nobody—
   I'm drinking, drinking, drinking!

But with each goblet that I drain
   My thirst grows big and bigger;
This is the case, I do maintain,
   With each true Rhine-wine swigger.
And yet I feel, come what come can,
   Whilst to the floor I'm sinking,
I've done my duty like a man
   In drinking, drinking, drinking!

K. MÜCHLER.

COMFORT AT PARTING.

'NEATH the moon that is waxing and waning
   We linger but for a day;
Swiftly our blooming-time fadeth
   With us from the world away.

Full many a troop of good fellows,
    Before us hath lived and laugh'd;
To the sleepers under the wild-flowers
    Be a beaker in memory quaff'd.

And many a troop of good fellows,
    Long after our bosoms are still,
To us sleeping under the wild-flowers
    Will beakers in memory fill.

We sit here so happy together,
    So lovingly live in our day;
And cheer up the world for each other—
    Ah, would we could live thus for aye!

Since vain is the wish, then let ever
    Warm love in our bosoms abide;
We know not how soon the fate cometh
    To scatter us far and wide.

And thus though long leagues stretch between us,
    Yet near will our fond hearts be;
And the joy of one will be ever
    A joy to you and to me.

And when our wanderings are over,
    Should friend once more meet friend;
Then a new and joyous beginning
    We'll knit to a jovial end.

        AUGUST FRIEDRICH FERDINAND VON KOTZEBUE.

FIDUCIT.

There were three boon companions,
  A merrie companie—
And gaily the wine-cup circled
  Among the trusty three.

They laugh'd and sang together—
  The lightest hearts on earth—
The world's grim cares and troubles
  Ne'er touch'd them in their mirth.

But Death call'd one unto him,
  Another follow'd fast;
And then the third sat lonely
  Where the hours of joy had pass'd.

Yet still as the time returnèd
  To drain the sparkling bowl,
He fill'd each brother's wine-cup,
  And sang with all his soul.

And once as he sang all lonely
  To the harp he loved so well,
A tear-drop glitter'd downward,
  And into his wine-cup fell.

'I drink ye a health, my brothers!
  Why so dumb and silent are ye?
Ah, what has the world to give now
  If none will be merry with me?'

The glasses clink'd, and sudden
　　　　Stood drain'd on the table then—
　'*Fiducit!* jovial brother!'—
　　　　He never drank again.
　　　　　　　　　　　STUDENTS' SONG.

CHATEAU BONCOURT.

I SHAKE my grey locks aweary,
　　And dream of the days of yore—
Ye scenes that I thought forgotten,
　　Why haunt me any more?

High out of a bowery covert
　　A castle glimmers in state,
I know the towers and turrets,
　　The old stone bridge, and the gate.

There from the old escutcheon
　　The lions look kindly on me;
I greet the dear old faces,
　　And into the courtyard flee.

There crouches the Sphinx by the fountain,—
　　I see my fig-tree gleam;
'Twas there behind that window
　　I dream'd sweet childhood's dream.

Softly I enter the chapel,
　　And come to my fathers' tomb;
There from the pillar beside it,
　　Their banner droops in gloom.

Bright through the colour'd window
  A gleam lights up the place,
But the words of the old inscription
  My dim eyes cannot trace.

And thus, O hall of my fathers,
  So true in my heart art thou!
Ah me! from the world thou 'st vanish'd,
  The plough goes over thee now.

Dear soil that I love, be fruitful;
  My blessing rest on each field;
To whomsoever ploughs thee
  Rich harvests ever yield!

But I will arise, and taking
  My harp into my hand,
Wide o'er the world I'll wander,
  And sing from land to land.

ADALBERT VON CHAMISSO.

TO THE FATHERLAND.

O FATHERLAND, though far thou art,
  Thou com'st to me in truth!
I think of thee as of the heart,
  The vanish'd heart of youth.

I stand alone and dream of thee,
  And gaze across the waves,
And my dreams mingle with the sea
  As nightly thus it raves.

And haply to my heart is brought
    Joy from the breakers' roar,
I listen dumb as if I caught
    Some tidings from thy shore.

Methinks I hear the breezes play
    About thy oaken bowers,
Where, musing, I would dream away
    The long sweet summer hours.

Let the dark seething billows rush,
    They tell of friends and thee,
For then I hear thy brooklets gush
    Reproachful calling me.

The tinkle of thy cattle-bells
    Once more methinks I hear;
Once more thy mountain-carol swells
    And thrills upon my ear.

Thy groves sigh'd at the parting time,
    The bird sang from the tree,
And every little leaf did chime,
    'Ah, wanderer! think of me,'—

What time beside the rolling flood
    To thy dear shore I clung,
While 'neath the linden-tree I stood
    And sad farewell I sung.

My tears fell fast, so loath to part!
    And 'neath that linden-tree,
Ah, fondly in my deepest heart
    I pledged my troth to thee.

Of thee, loved land, I fondly think,
  Thou hast the friends I know;
To thee by darkling ocean's brink
  My warm tears ever flow.

NICOLAUS LENAU.

RHINE SONG.

My heart's with the Rhine! O thou dearly-loved strand!
My heart's with the Rhine of my own native land!
Where my youth glided past, where the kind faces be,
Where my loved one is blooming and thinking of me,
Where I have been merry with music and wine—
Wherever I wander my heart's with the Rhine!

I greet thee, thou broad glancing river! still roam
By castle and hamlet, by city and dome.
Thou bright golden grain in the soft swelling vale,
Ye woods and rough crags and dark gorges I hail!
And you, sunny hill-slopes, where gleameth the vine!—
Wherever I wander my heart's with the Rhine!

I greet ye, old times! and ah fondly I muse
On the songs and the wassail and frolicsome crews!
I greet thee, brave race! and I greet thee again,
For fair are thy women, and true are thy men!
O'er thy path through the world may the sun ever shine!
Wherever I wander my heart's with the Rhine!

My heart's with the Rhine! O thou dearly-loved strand!
My heart's with the Rhine of my own native land!

Where my youth glided past, where the kind faces be—
Where my loved one is blooming and thinking of me—
Unchanged thus remain! and be mine, still be mine!
Wherever I wander my heart's with the Rhine!

WOLFGANG MÜLLER.

Imitations.

IMITATIONS.

TO NELL.

Butterflies, butterflies, tell me true,
Is there aught so fair in the world as you?—
Aught so brimming with innocent mirth,
As ye dance about o'er the laughing earth?

Wild-flowers, wild-flowers, fretted with dew,
Is there aught so tender and gentle as you?
So trustful, so true, methinks ye were given
For types of the angel-life in heaven.

Little bird, little bird, where shall we meet
With love so pure as thy notes repeat?—
With love so joyous and bright and strong?—
Thy life is only a beautiful song.

Yes! lightsome and gay as the dainty things
That flutter about on golden wings;
And tender and gentle and trustful and true
As the little flowers all fretted with dew;

And full of love as the little bird
Whose song in the summer sky is heard;
And dearer to me than tongue can tell
Or heart can think is my own sweet Nell.

DOWN WHERE THE ASPENS QUIVER.

Down where the aspens quiver
   I nightly take my rest,
And whisper to the river
   With the stars upon its breast.

I sigh for the golden blisses
   Of which the roses dream,
I scatter many kisses
   Upon the glancing stream.

The dew-drop comes to the blossom,
   And sleep to the bird on the tree;
But, ah! my love-lorn bosom,
   No balm will come to thee.

Where the broadening river glistens
   In the moonlight far away,
A maiden stoops and listens
   To the wavelets' roundelay.

They sing of a bootless battle,
   Of love and a lovelorn breast;
And, mix'd with their own sweet prattle,
   Come yearning sighs for rest.

The maiden caught the kisses
   As they floated down the stream,
And dream'd of golden blisses
   Such as the roses dream;

And bending low, she blushes,
    And breathes a balm for me —
But ah! the river rushes
    Down to the desolate sea.

LUX NATURÆ.

LONG ago when my heart was young
Life was a lamp with diamonds hung.
O the golden light it shed abroad
Made earth a heaven and man a god!

Then the secret song of my soul I heard
In the fall of the wave and the song of the bird;
And the mystic thoughts no tongue may tell
Were breathed back to me in a dewy dell.

Does the light burn dim? does my heart grow cold?
Do I dream as I dreamt in the days of old?
Have shadows fallen where the light was thrown,
And time crept o'er me like moss on a stone?

Shall this world of beauty bloom no more
With a purple glory as of yore?
Must the flowers be dumb, and the birds and streams
Utter no more my secret dreams?

Away! away! for the sun is up,
And the dewdrop faints in its azure cup;
The mists of the morning dissolve in light,
And music rings out from the crystal height.

And lo! again in field and fell
Glimmer the thoughts no tongue may tell;
A secret spirit breathes through the whole
And trembles softly to my soul.

And ah! whate'er may await me in time,
I ne'er shall forget this golden prime:
'Twill brighten the glance of the sinking light,
And gleam on the curtains of the night.

www.ingramcontent.com/pod-product-compliance
Lightning Source LLC
Chambersburg PA
CBHW020910230426
43666CB00008B/1398